Do you ever get the feeling that, despite all your misgivings, there is something you really must do? Reading all the Old Testament part of the Bible is like that for many people. We have no enthusiasm for it, because it is so long, complicated, out of date and beyond our understanding. Well, despair no longer, for help is at hand. Chris Sinkinson has written this marvellous book to give us all the help we need in understanding the big picture and developing a desire for the first part of the Bible. We travel through time with a Doctor who needs no Tardis to help us traverse the various places we will visit. He will show and explain to us many strange and wonderful things. So get on board and enjoy the experience of *Time Travel to the Old Testament*.

—*Clive Anderson, minister, tour leader and author, co-author of* Through the British Museum with the Bible

Chris Sinkinson brings to life the sights, sounds and culture of the Old Testament world, giving readers a valuable opportunity to enter into seemingly familiar stories and explore their riches in a fresh way. Informative, yet very readable, this book is a great resource for those who want to begin to study the Scriptures in context, gaining a deeper understanding of the biblical story and the roots of the Christian faith.

—*Heidi Johnston, speaker, and author of* Life in the Big Story

In an easy style, Chris Sinkinson shows how the books of the Old Testament are realistic and relevant for today. Without avoiding difficulties, he demonstrates how modern archaeological discoveries aid understanding of the Bible.

—*Alan Millard, Emeritus Rankin Professor of Hebrew and Ancient Semitic Languages, The University of Liverpool*

We live in a day when Bible knowledge cannot be assumed. In general, children are largely untaught the Bible, and those who come to faith in their teens or later (as so many do) have a major task on their hands. For such, Dr Sinkinson's book will shine as a bright beacon. When I say that he skips his merry way through a remarkably full summary of Old Testament life, thought, history and context, I do not imply superficiality but call attention to an enviable lightness of touch and style in a book that nourishes heart and head alike.

—*Alec Motyer, author and Bible expositor*

With carefully researched facts and enjoyable wit, Sinkinson invites his readers into the real history of the Hebrew Bible. He helps followers of Jesus Christ remember that the story of Abraham, Isaac, Samson, and David is their story too; they follow the same God and should be familiar with his work throughout history. I commend this book to you, as I believe it will add to Christians' understanding of the world of the Old Testament, and of the God who creates and redeems our world through his Son.

—*Jon Nielson, College Pastor, College Church, Wheaton*

I've suffered from some travel guides over the years. They know too much and bore you by going on and on. But Chris Sinkinson proves a wonderful guide to the long-ago world of the Old Testament: sure-footed, interesting, and dispensing up-to-date knowledge with a light and humorous touch. He's aware of just how much we need to know to make sense of what we read. Under his expert teaching so much that seems difficult is opened up. The book is 'simply wonderful'—and both words are important.

—*Derek Tidball, former Principal, London School of Theology*

TIME TRAVEL

to the

OLD TESTAMENT

An Essential Companion for

the Christian Explorer

CHRIS SINKINSON

PUBLISHING

P.O. BOX 817 • PHILLIPSBURG • NEW JERSEY 08865-0817

First published in the UK by Inter-Varsity Press in 2013 under the title *Time Travel to the Old Testament: Your Essential Companion*

North American edition issued 2014 by P&R Publishing

Unless otherwise stated, Scripture quotations are taken from the Holy Bible, New International Version® Anglicized, NIV® Copyright © 1979, 1984, 2011 by Biblica, Inc.® Used by permission. All rights reserved worldwide.

Scripture quotation from the New Living Translation is taken from the Holy Bible, New Living Translation, copyright ©1996, 2004, 2007, 2013 by Tyndale House Foundation. Used by permission of Tyndale House Publishers, Inc., Carol Stream, Illinois 60188. All rights reserved.

ISBN: 978-1-59638-984-7 (pbk)
ISBN: 978-1-59638-985-4 (ePub)
ISBN: 978-1-59638-986-1 (Mobi)

Printed in the United States of America

Library of Congress Cataloging-in-Publication Data

Sinkinson, Christopher.
   Time travel to the Old Testament : an essential companion for the Christian explorer / Chris Sinkinson. -- 1st North American Edition.
      pages cm
Includes bibliographical references and index.
ISBN 978-1-59638-984-7 (pbk.)
1. Bible. Old Testament--Introductions. I. Title.
BS1140.3.S56 2014
221.6'1--dc23

                                    2014010441

Dedicated to the students at Moorlands College,
for encouraging a tutor to continue to learn

CONTENTS

List of illustrations		9
Acknowledgments		11
1.	Preparing to embark	15
2.	Hebrew storytelling	33
3.	On location	53
4.	Going back to our roots	69
5.	Meet the natives	87
6.	Among many gods	109
7.	Laying down the law	131
8.	War and peace	151
9.	Back to the future	173
	Further reading	189
	Notes	193
	Scripture index	203
	General index	205

ILLUSTRATIONS

1. Timeline: The Old Testament story   12
2. Map of ancient Israel's natural features   13
3. Map of the Fertile Crescent   14
4. Qumran cave © Mike Brookbank   29
5. Pleiades © NASA, ESA, and AURA/Caltech   64
6. Rock badger © Chris Sinkinson   66
7. Mountain goat (ibex) © Mike Brookbank   66
8. Jericho stone tower © Mike Brookbank   78
9. Ziggurat of Ur: original ruins (1960)
    © Alan Millard   91
10. Reconstruction of the Ziggurat of Ur
    © Ricardo Cook Martins   91
11. Rosetta Stone – Wikimedia Commons,
    © Hans Hillewaert/CC-BY-SA-3.0   93
12. Scarab seal © Chris Sinkinson   95
13. Settler in Canaan (Public domain)   99
14. The shrine at Dan © Chris Sinkinson   100
15. Black Obelisk detail – Wikimedia Commons,
    © Steven G. Johnson/CC-BY-SA-3.0   103
16. Akhenaten © Keith Schengili-Roberts   115
17. Baby cemetery © Alan Millard   117

18. Dome of the Rock © Chris Sinkinson 127
19. Map of the exodus 154
20. Stones from Hazor © Mike Brookbank 157
21. Stones from Hazor © Mike Brookbank 157
22. Reconstruction of gates © Ricardo Cook Martins 163
23. Assyrian soldiers – Wikimedia Commons, © MikePeel/www.mikepeel.net 166
24. Warrior with sling © Martin Doyle 166
25. Sumerian chariots (Public domain) 167
26. Rameses II chariot (Public domain) 168
27. Assyrian siege engine (Public domain) 171

ACKNOWLEDGMENTS

I am very grateful for the many people who have helped me to feel at home in the world of the Old Testament. Bible teachers like Rupert Bentley-Taylor and Dale Ralph Davis have made the text live as I have heard their sermons. For comment on the manuscript, I am particularly grateful to Professor Alan Millard and Clive Anderson, and to Marie and Andre Moubarak of Twin Tours in Israel. The students at Moorlands College are my persistent assistants in listening to my own teaching material and helping me see things more clearly. The good people at IVP have helped to shape this manuscript, particularly Eleanor Trotter and Kath Stanton. Kev Jones has enthusiastically given his design skills to this project. Any mistakes remaining in the text are my responsibility!

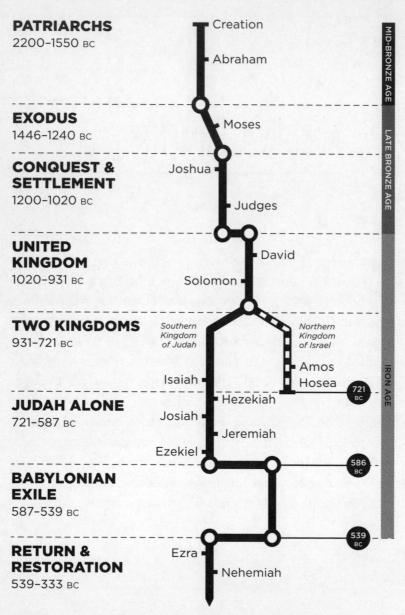

PATRIARCHS
2200–1550 BC

Creation

Abraham

EXODUS
1446–1240 BC

Moses

**CONQUEST &
SETTLEMENT**
1200–1020 BC

Joshua

Judges

**UNITED
KINGDOM**
1020–931 BC

David

Solomon

TWO KINGDOMS
931–721 BC

*Southern
Kingdom
of Judah*

*Northern
Kingdom
of Israel*

Amos
Hosea

Isaiah

721
BC

JUDAH ALONE
721–587 BC

Hezekiah

Josiah

Jeremiah

Ezekiel

**BABYLONIAN
EXILE**
587–539 BC

586
BC

**RETURN &
RESTORATION**
539–333 BC

539
BC

Ezra

Nehemiah

MID-BRONZE AGE

LATE BRONZE AGE

IRON AGE

TIMELINE: THE OLD TESTAMENT STORY

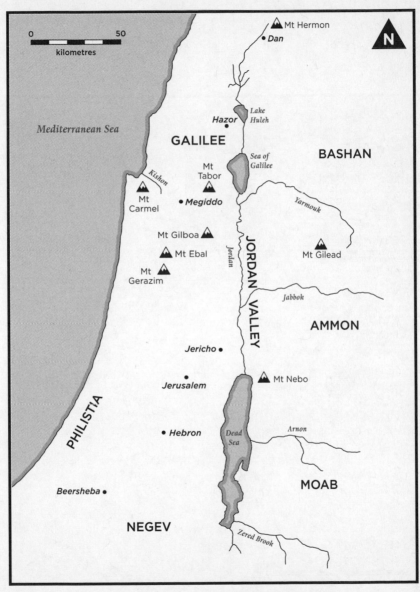

0   50
kilometres

N

Mt Hermon

Dan

Mediterranean Sea

Lake Huleh

Hazor

GALILEE

Sea of Galilee

BASHAN

Mt Tabor

Kishon

Mt Carmel

Megiddo

Yarmouk

Mt Gilboa

Mt Ebal

Jordan

Mt Gilead

Mt Gerazim

JORDAN VALLEY

Jabbok

AMMON

Jericho

Jerusalem

Mt Nebo

Hebron

Dead Sea

Arnon

PHILISTIA

Beersheba

MOAB

NEGEV

Zered Brook

MAP OF ANCIENT ISRAEL'S NATURAL FEATURES

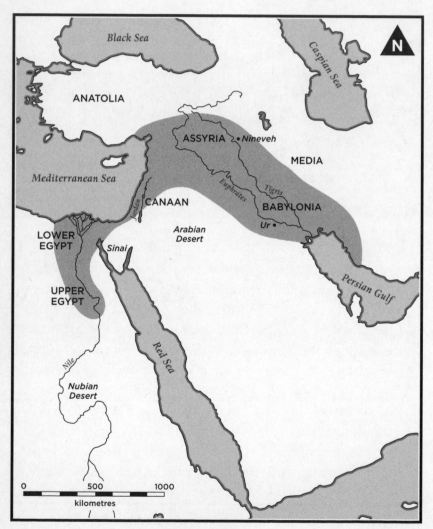

Black Sea

Caspian Sea

ANATOLIA

ASSYRIA · Nineveh

MEDIA

Mediterranean Sea

Euphrates

Tigris

BABYLONIA

CANAAN

Jordan

Arabian
Desert

Ur ·

LOWER
EGYPT

Sinai

Persian Gulf

UPPER
EGYPT

Red Sea

Nile

Nubian
Desert

0   500   1000

kilometres

MAP OF THE FERTILE CRESCENT

1

PREPARING TO EMBARK

If I could turn back time

I hardly need to tell you that time travel remains a favoured theme of science fiction writers. From H. G. Wells's *The Time Machine* to Audrey Niffenegger's *The Time Traveller's Wife* more than a century later, our appetites for stories that bend the rules of the universe have shown no sign of abating. Perhaps for some, watching *Doctor Who* simply reveals a love of fantasy and adventure. But I have a feeling that, for everyone, there is a deeply held wish to move outside the boundaries of time. We would like to see what it was like to have lived in the past, marched with a Roman army, viewed the building of the pyramids or listened to the philosopher Socrates as he taught his disciples. Particularly with the benefit of a route back to the present, I doubt if anyone would turn down the opportunity to take a trip in that famous blue police box.

For religious people, there is an added reason for this desire. Most of the major world religions were founded long ago and relate to events in ancient history. Did those miracles really happen? What were those religious founders actually like? And, given how much a religion influences present life, how important is it for us to be sure that we have not been mistaken or misled?

For Christians and Jews, the books described variously as the Old Testament or the Hebrew Bible provide a rich itinerary for the would-be time traveller. What happened in and around the land called Canaan in the ancient world? Who were the Israelites, and did God really speak to them?

There is good news. Time travel is possible. At least, with a bit of communication from the past and imagination in the present, we can enter the world of ancient history. This kind of time travelling has been going on since people first learned how to write down their thoughts and histories. And the people of the ancient world have travelled into the future too—we still hear their words today.

Keys to the past

So here are the tools for a Christian time traveller. First, a Bible. We are going to explore the ancient world of the Israelites through their records. This will involve carefully considering the meaning of what they wrote, thereby avoiding superficial interpretations. Secondly, we will need an imagination. We don't just read their words as if they wrote them yesterday. We recognize the need to take an imaginative leap into another place and time. We are not imagining things that are *not* there, but things that *are* there. By using our imagination, we gain sympathy and empathy with the characters. We start to see things a little like they did and understand a little better what their world looked like.

However, the tools of Bible and imagination need to be supplemented by other guides. There is the important issue of language. Three languages are evident in the Bible: Hebrew, Aramaic and Greek. To understand the text, we will need either a brilliant, personal grasp of these languages or an accurate translation. Thankfully for non-linguists, accurate translations are easily accessible![1] Then there is the issue of geographical and historical context. What do we know from outside the Bible that will help us understand the numerous references to places and events from the ancient world? The fact is that we know a great deal, and much of this will enrich our grasp of the Bible.

These additional guides are not hard to find. Exploring the world of the ancient Israelites is not the preserve of experts. With a little assistance, anyone can do it. Indeed, even without knowledge of biblical languages or the archaeology of the Ancient Near East, any thoughtful reader can still make plenty of headway. They can understand the main plot of the Old Testament and grasp the meaning of the individual stories. This is what Christians mean by a doctrine called 'the perspicuity of Scripture'. This doctrine affirms that the Bible is not essentially very complex and mysterious, but deliberately clear and accessible. If it is the Word of God, then that is exactly what we should expect. Not a book that is intentionally hard to understand, but writings that aim to be understood and convey important information to future generations.

However, the perspicuity of Scripture does not imply that this is always easy, or that everything in Scripture is equally clear, or that we will never get confused. After all, even the apostle Peter said this of the New Testament letters of Paul: 'His letters contain some things that are hard to understand' (2 Peter 3:16). So we should be encouraged, both that the Bible is not being deliberately obscure and that even people far more knowledgeable than we struggled at times!

The last thing I want to do is make the Bible seem more complex to you than it seemed at first. I want us to make use of any and every helpful guide to unlock its meaning. But I also want to be clear that this can be a demanding process. Sometimes we forget or ignore just how different the ancient world can be. Let's face it, those who try reading the Bible from cover to cover, starting in Genesis, often get bogged down by about Leviticus in a system of obscure sacrificial rules and regulations that have little apparent bearing on our lives today.

Obstacles in our way

How many factors conspire to make the Old Testament, in particular, seem obscure to us? There are a number, and I will elaborate on a few here.

Places can seem strange to us, even if we have a modern Hebrew background. Take, for example: 'Now Abraham moved on from there into the region of the Negev and lived between Kadesh and Shur. For a while he stayed in Gerar . . .' (Genesis 20:1). Exactly where are these places and why do they matter? Too many unusual names or locations, and the text quickly becomes a little blurred. We will tend to skim-read the words. But what if we can identify those places? And what if we can imagine what it is like to stand in the hot, parched Negev desert, knowing that we are not among the rolling sand dunes of the Sahara, but among the grey rocks and chalky canyons of southern Israel? What if we know that the Hebrew word 'Negev' shares a common root with the word for dryness? Then we know that this is a desert where it is possible, though difficult, to eke out a living. A little rain in the winter is enough to ensure that flowers will bloom there in the spring, and the stunted acacia trees will slowly grow, resisting the intense heat of the day and the cold of the night. With this kind of background knowledge, places quickly come to life, and we find that simple Bible words carry us far away from the park bench where we are reading them.

The **legal codes** of the Old Testament are particularly perplexing. OK, so some, like most of the Ten Commandments, will seem quite obvious. Do we really need to be told not to steal, for example? But others take us by surprise: 'Do not wear clothes of wool and linen woven together. Make tassels on the four corners of the cloak you wear' (Deuteronomy 22:11–12). Try as I might, it is hard to shop at the local supermarket and avoid some kind of polyester mix, and even harder to source something with tassels on each corner. Of course, it is easy just to ignore these words and skate over them, muttering, 'These words don't apply to us today.' But why don't we say that about the command not to steal? And even if some don't apply to us today, why on earth did they apply to the Israelites at that time? I would not have wanted my neighbour to be a thief, but why would I have worried about his sense of fashion?

However, if I had read my Old Testament more widely, I might have remembered that God explained to Moses that a tassel on the hem of a garment was never a fashion statement: 'You will have these tassels to look at and so you will remember all the commands of the LORD, that you may obey them' (Numbers 15:39). With that reference in mind, I can now imagine an Israelite considering those tassels a pleasure, a physical aid to remembering that the whole of life is lived in worship. I can imagine him standing in a crowded marketplace, waiting to buy from a stall, curling those tassels in his fingers. It looks as if he is just fidgeting in impatience. But perhaps he is being reminded of the commands of God. As his fingers touch the tassels, he remembers that it is good to pay properly for goods bought at the market stall, and not to steal or cheat, for this is what pleases the Lord. We worship God at the checkout, as much as in the chapel. Don't those tassels make a little more sense now? And might this not cast some light on why people wanted to touch the fringe or hem of Jesus' garment (Matthew 14:36)? As for the prohibition on mixed fabrics, we will return to that in chapter 7, but obscure laws on mould, eggs, pigs and snakes may leave us bewildered.

But perhaps the greatest obstacle to our appreciation of the ancient world is its apparent **barbarity and violence**. Indeed, the Hebrew Bible raises some perplexing moral issues. Provision for a slave trade, the treatment of women and the way the land of Canaan was captured all present difficult questions. While the fall of Jericho to the marching band of Israel might seem like a suitable story for a children's Sunday school talk, a closer look at the details makes it clear that this is adult-rated material. The destruction of the walls and the death of the inhabitants cause some to dismiss these events as examples of genocide. It leads to the almost proverbial saying that the God of the Old Testament was a God of wrath and anger, replaced by the New Testament God of love and mercy. But such a distinction is deeply misleading. The God revealed in the New Testament remains a God who will bring judgment (Acts 5:9–11; 1 Corinthians 11:29–30; 2 Thessalonians 1:6–9, Revelation 20:11–12). There is no need to drive a wedge between the Testaments, but moral issues remain that can leave us feeling distinctly ill at ease.

And **poems** can be confusing. Imagery and poetry rely on shared conventions to draw our emotions and feelings into what we read. A simple metaphor, 'Love is blind,' can communicate a great deal. Generally, we know when we are reading a poem or a newspaper article. Within those different texts, we can distinguish between a literal description and an emotive metaphor. But when we travel back in time to the ancient world of the Israelites, these distinctions are harder to make. What is Genesis chapter 1? Is it an extended psalm or a poem? Is it a historical or scientific record of creation? When we turn to a book like the Song of Songs, we easily recognize it as a form of love poetry rather than a historical book. But what do the images and metaphors mean? When I was courting my wife, never once did I describe her teeth as being like 'a flock of sheep just shorn', or her neck 'like the tower of David, built with courses of stone; on it hang a thousand shields' (Songs of Songs 4:2–4). I'm not sure she would have been best pleased if I had done.

Other obstacles to seeing the world through the eyes of an ancient Israelite include the **complexity of Old Testament history** and the **odd behaviour of some of its heroes**. If Samson really is such a man of faith, why does he sleep with a prostitute? And how can a Spirit-anointed leader of Israel be so completely stupid? Doesn't he realize that Delilah is just trying to get him killed, or does he think it's a coincidence that her friends keep trying to murder him?

History or mythology?

So the Bible can be a very strange place. But it can also be very familiar. For all the problems above, there are many things that we can relate to. The Bible's concern with time and place still matters to us. When we are told that Abraham travels to the oak trees of Mamre (Genesis 18:1), we may not be sure where that is, but we can imagine the oak trees. We get the sense of a real person travelling to a real place among real vegetation. With some careful study and reflection, the Old Testament can become a portal leading into the very real world of ancient history.

History is an important word. It describes a science of recording events and making sense of them in a coherent narrative. The classical Greek writer Herodotus (c.484–420 BC) was named the 'father' of modern history by Cicero. However, the Bible lays claim to being history too. This is a striking fact because religious texts in the ancient world did not normally lay claim to being historical. They were generally a type of literature called mythology, and a myth can be a story or epic tale of great inspirational significance, but not one set in time and place.

Early creation epics from the Ancient Near East, or the long religious epics of Hindu literature, like the Bhagavad Gita, do not share this concern with historical dates. Yes, they are great stories that reflect universal themes, but they lay no claim to historical accuracy.

Myths do not generally come in the form of a linear account of events. By contrast, the Old Testament offers a linear story, which begins at the beginning, pursues an ancestral line down through the centuries and ties into the more recent history of the first century AD. In fact, while the history of God's revelation in Scripture ceased around the time of the death of the last apostle, history itself continues. There are history books that will pick up where Luke left off at the end of the book of Acts and continue the story towards the present. While these are not part of the Bible as revelation, such books are continuing historical accounts, sharing similar concerns with many of the Bible writers.

It is fashionable to point out that it's naïve to assume the Old Testament to be historical. Inexplicable miracles, alleged contradictions and Hebrew folk tales are all used as evidence. We should, we are told, enjoy the Old Testament as literature, much as we would a work of fantasy, rather than imagining it as a historical textbook.

But this objection itself is naïve. It relies on a false dichotomy, in which we must choose between the Bible as history or the Bible as fiction. Without question, some of the Old Testament is not in the style of a historical textbook— there are songs, poems, proverbs and parables scattered throughout. But a song can still convey historical information, and it must have a social setting in which it was composed and sung.

The objection can also be a distraction. By discussing which stories are historical and which are parable, we can quickly lose sight of a more obvious bigger picture, which is that the Old Testament has a linear, historical movement from creation to new creation.

However old the universe may be, it did have a beginning. The earth was formed, and Adam and Eve were created from the dust of the ground. The process described in Genesis 1–2 provides an opening for the epic story of Scripture. The initial state of Adam and Eve in the garden of Eden is one of harmony and purpose. There is work to be done and a world to be explored. Within the garden grows the tree of life, which ensures an everlasting life, and the visible presence of the God who can walk there in the cool of the day. Eve is mother of the living, and all people will be able to lay claim to her as their ancestor.

Adam and Eve's disobedience in the garden leads to the event described by Christians as 'the fall'. When they are tempted by the mysterious talking serpent into eating from the tree of the knowledge of good and evil, the relationship between them and God is broken. They leave the garden, the tree of life and the visible presence of God. Life east of Eden will be hard and painful, and will lead to death.

The family trees of Genesis may be dull reading, but they are important for giving us the sense of a flowing history: a genealogy for the peoples of the ancient world. This is not intended to be comprehensive and it leaves many unanswered questions, but it does have direction. History is on the move. We watch old people die and new children arrive. The importance of following a family tree may reflect the heads-up we were given by God's words at the fall. He promised Eve that, for all the damage the serpent had done, the solution would come from her own descendants. Speaking to the serpent, God says,

> I will put enmity
>   between you and the woman,
>   and between your offspring and hers;
> he will crush your head,
>   and you will strike his heel.
> (Genesis 3:15)

Exactly who is this mysterious serpent crusher? Do these words simply describe a never-ending struggle between the human race and poisonous snakes, or are they referring to a cosmic conflict between the descendants of Eve and the forces of evil? At this stage, we are not told, but we are being directed to watch the linear flow of history, as we leave the garden far behind.[2]

So how do we relate this account of history to the secular historical timelines evident in museums and referenced by television documentaries?

'Prehistory' refers to the time when historical records were not being kept. The dominant material technology was stone, so it was also called 'the Stone Age'. In some ways this is a misnomer, as the people of this time actually used a lot more wood than stone and also had access to some metals. But stone is more durable than wood, and so Stonehenge is better preserved than the Woodhenge that preceded it. Stone flints and axes can be found in abundance. And forget those images of bearded men grunting to one another in ignorance. There is evidence of culture, art, civilization and intellectual thought from the Stone Age. It may not be quite Fred Flintstone, but neither is it a story of barbaric savages. However, because we have no written records, we can only guess at what was happening among these people. The opening chapters of Genesis cast light on a prehistoric setting, beyond the reach of secular historians.

However, from the time of Abraham onwards, we find ourselves in the historic period. Developments like bronze, and later iron, aided technological change. But the development of writing and the invention of the alphabet may be even more important still. Written records from across the ancient world preserve information that helps us understand not just historical events, but the lives of ordinary people too. Carved on stone and inscribed in clay is the information that forms the basis for what we call history. Reading the Bible, we witness the linear development of a people over time.

Abraham lives as a nomadic shepherd in the wild lands of Canaan during the Bronze Age. Moses, a later descendant of Abraham, becomes an important figure in what is called the New Kingdom of Egypt, long after the time of the pyramid builders. The exodus of the Israelites from Egypt and the settlement of the Promised Land took place during an important period of technological change. We move from a time known as the Late Bronze Age into the Early Iron Age.

To understand why this matters, we will need to understand something of the significance of these metals.

Bronze is a good, hard metal, so bronze artefacts from the ancient world survived well. It is an 'alloy', or mixture, of copper and tin. How anyone got the idea of mixing these two metals we do not know, but it gave them a strong, malleable metal for making tools and weapons. However, the discovery of iron was a step even further forward. There was a kind of iron that humans had known about since the Stone Age, one that could be found in meteorites. But it was only of limited value. To refine the kind of iron useful for tools and weapons, humans had to work out how to generate enormous temperatures in ovens. And, with enough regulated heat, iron could be smelted and bent to all kinds of purposes.

Iron tools and weapons allow for sharper points and lighter equipment, so an army using iron weapons would have a clear advantage over one relying on bronze.

As the Israelites begin to settle in the land, they arrive as a Bronze Age people. But another group are arriving who are technologically more advanced. The Philistines had begun to make use of iron, and this seems to have given them the upper hand. We will find on our journey that this kind of reference to wider world history will help us make sense of what we discover in the Bible.

As time goes by

The ancient world is marked by empires that rose and fell, and were in time replaced by successors. The Egyptians, Assyrians and Babylonians all take turns at controlling the region of Canaan. During their rise and fall, the descendants of Abraham continue to multiply, appointing kings and forming alliances. And the books of the Bible fit with these different periods.

Some Bible books are obviously in the genre of annals or chronicles of history. Others, like collections of psalms or proverbs, are not historical writings in that sense, but they still have a cultural setting within that historical flow. The psalms that David wrote do not belong to the period of Abraham, and their images and ideas would be misunderstood if we misplaced them in time. Judges belongs to the earliest of these times, when Egypt dominated the region, and 2 Kings will witness the much later fall of Assyria and the rise of Babylon. The book of Daniel will chart the decline of Babylon, and Ezra will take place in the new world order of the Persians.

As the Old Testament draws to a close, the Israelites are only a small rump of a people group, with a territory that is rarely independent of the control of other powers. It will pass from the Persians, to the Greeks, to the Romans, and so the social historical backdrop for the Gospels will be significantly different from that of the Old Testament. Greek and Roman culture have little bearing on our interpretation of Old Testament literature, but they are certainly pivotal in our interpretation of the New Testament. After the collapse of the Roman Empire, other powers will arise and show an interest in this historic land, even right down to the modern age. This forms the backdrop to the modern tensions and struggles, for we cannot understand global contemporary politics without understanding the ancient religious traditions.

So the Old Testament follows a linear timeline, with a beginning, a middle and a journey towards an end. For the Christian reader, that end has not yet been reached, but it is glimpsed in the vision of John called the book of Revelation.

All this shows that the Bible is not a mythical fairy tale set outside time and place. Whether people believe it to be accurate or not, it was written with attention to historical changes and an unfolding plot. This kind of history writing is sometimes called 'historiography', and many scholars identify aspects of the records that are far from neutral or unbiased accounts. The writing reflects the concerns of the authors and makes moral judgments on the events described. Sometimes this is dismissed as pre-critical propaganda, but such an objection is unfair. The Bible never claims to be a neutral history of Israel or world events. It is prejudiced in favour of a divine perspective on history. And is that such a bad thing? To turn this point around, can *any* historical writing avoid all bias or prejudice? The modern historian claiming objectivity must also be selective in what he or she chooses to record or ignore, and must also make judgments about what matters. History is not a view from nowhere, but a view from some particular window on the world.

So the Bible has a timeline, and no time traveller should leave home without it. This timeline helps us to locate ourselves in history. Unless we grasp where events and characters fit into it, we will misunderstand the stories. We may find universal truths, but we will miss their key place in one unfolding story. And the timeline will also help us relate secular history to what we read.

Trusting the transport

Everything we have said so far is built on one important assumption: that the Bible is a reliable text for discovering history. Can we trust it for this purpose? Furthermore, can we be sure that the text we are using has not been distorted over the centuries? If errors crept in 500 years ago, then what hope is there for us accessing the history of 3,000 years ago?

These two objections are not to be lightly dismissed. The first concerns the content of the Bible: is it an accurate record? The second concerns the transmission of the Bible: has it been reliably copied? Thankfully, we can answer both of these questions with a resounding 'yes'.

Regarding the first objection, the Old Testament has consistently been shown to be a reliable guide in those areas where it can actually be tested. The accounts of personalities and conflicts are often corroborated by sources outside the Bible. Some events that we read about are also described by non-biblical writers or have even left material remains in the archaeological record. Of course, the further back we go, the less evidence remains, but there is still enough to remind us that we are dealing with some form of history, even in its earliest writings.

The second objection, that the Bible may have been corrupted over the years, can easily be tested. There is a vast number of manuscripts and fragments going back over centuries that we can compare with the manuscripts we use today. These comparisons enable us to state categorically that Jewish scribal tradition had a genuine commitment to preserving the text, even when it might have been tempting to revise or rewrite it. The discovery of the Dead Sea Scrolls from

Cave 4 at Qumran near the Dead Sea, where many of the longer scrolls were found.

about 1947 onwards provided us with material remains of Scriptures copied over 1,000 years earlier than some of those known at the time. A solid confirmation of the reliability of the copying process.

However, for a Christian there is an even more fundamental reason for trusting the Old Testament Scriptures and spending time in that ancient world, namely that this is the world from which Jesus came. The nation of Israel provided the context for his ministry. He was born a Jew, knew the Hebrew Scriptures and was brought up in its traditions and theology. The New Testament itself assumes this backdrop and is in many ways a commentary on the Old Testament and its relationship to Jesus Christ. Jesus brought the promises and expectations of the Old Testament to fulfilment, but did not devalue its words in the process: 'In the past God spoke to our ancestors through the prophets at many times and in various ways, but in these last days he has spoken to us by his Son' (Hebrews 1:1–2). Open any New Testament book and start counting the references to the Old Testament. Nowhere are those writings devalued or downgraded, but everywhere we find them held up as true, as having authority and as being directly relevant to the follower of Christ.[3]

Many Christians carry around a slim New Testament volume. It is a practical item, fitting easily into a pocket or backpack. It doesn't seem so heavy or religious. When a new believer wants to start reading the Bible, we usually suggest they start with the Gospels rather than in Genesis. All very sensible, but it's a temporary measure. Sooner rather than later, we will need to immerse ourselves in the Hebrew Bible, upon which the New Testament is founded. Not to do so is to risk stunted growth and a shallow faith. I know it can seem a strange place at first, but the Old Testament is our home. So as we travel back in time, we won't find ourselves moving further into obscurity, but further into clarity and a deeper understanding of our New Testament faith.

Bible field trip

Reading: Genesis 1:1–2:3
Date: Creation
Destination: Planet Earth

1. What truths about creation do we learn from this chapter?

2. How would you describe God's relationship to creation?

3. What is the purpose of humankind in this creation (1:26–30)?

4. See Revelation 21:1–4 and 22:1–5 to glimpse a regenerated creation.

2

HEBREW STORYTELLING

We all love stories. As we travel in our time machine, we will discover that some of the oldest literary records from around the world are stories, myths and legends.

The Israelites loved stories too. It has been estimated that as much as 40 percent of the Old Testament is in the form of story or narrative. Why are stories so popular? Because they record history in a way that is enjoyable to hear. Not only that, but stories are memorable. They engage our imagination and emotions. If you are a reader of novels, then you will often have had the experience of being so caught up in the story that you do not really see the pages of the book any more. For a moment, it is as if you are *in* the story and not merely deciphering a written text.

So it should not surprise us that stories form such a large part of the Hebrew Bible. History has been recorded for us in memorable stories, to which we can relate. When publishers produce children's Bibles, they generally select the more arresting stories, illustrate them and package them as an edited Bible. And these are often 100 percent narrative. So the first things that children will remember are not psalms or law codes or prophetic decrees. They will remember a man who got thrown into a den of lions or a boy who knocked down a giant with his sling.

It has always been this way. If you had been among those Hebrew refugees of the exodus, you would have been familiar with storytelling. Every night, they told stories under the desert stars. Once a year, you would have taken part in the Passover meal with your neighbours. By eating roasted lamb and bitter herbs, and flatbread made without yeast, you shared in edible reminders of the Passover. The whole family was present, and the instructions emphasized the place of children in it all. For, naturally, the curious preparations and menu for this annual meal provoked questions: 'And when your children ask you, "What does this ceremony mean to you?" then tell them . . .' (Exodus 12:26–27). Here children were to be seen *and* heard. The meal was an opportunity to tell the story of the Passover, how God had brought judgment on Egypt and deliverance to the Israelites.[1]

Story and history

We know that Christians can feel threatened by this emphasis on story. Remember our theme in chapter 1, that the Bible is essentially a history. From Genesis to Revelation, it is the history of God's unfolding purposes for people, and the family trees connect individuals from the ancient past to the time of Jesus. But when we hear an event in the Bible being discussed as a 'story', we feel that its historical value is under threat. However, this reaction is misguided. Stories may be history, and history is a story. As is often pointed out, history is 'his story', the story of God's dealings with the world.

Robert Alter, a Jewish theologian particularly influential in calling for a return to reading, and enjoying, the stories of the Hebrew Bible, comments,

> Let me hasten to say that in giving weight to fictionality, I do not mean to discount the historical impulse that informs the Hebrew Bible. The God of Israel, as so often has been observed, is above all the God of history: the working out of His purposes in history is a process that compels the attention of the Hebrew imagination, which is thus led to the most vital interest in the concrete and differential character of historical events.[2]

So is the Old Testament a book of stories or a book of history? Actually, it could be both. Alter describes the stories as 'fictionalized history'. This is a somewhat ambiguous term. Does the emphasis lie upon *fiction* or upon *history*?

If we are asking whether all the stories in the Bible are history, then we must answer 'no'. There are parables (2 Samuel 12:1–4), lies (2 Samuel 1:6–10), dreams (Genesis 41:1–7) and apocalyptic visions (Daniel 10). So how do we know when a story is history and when it is a parable? Generally, the distinction is not all that difficult to make. There are clues in the text itself. We are told, for example, that the story Nathan told David was a parable (2 Samuel 12:7). We are told that a lie was told in 2 Samuel 1 because what really happened had already been reported (1 Samuel 31). We are told that Daniel had a vision (Daniel 10:1), and that Pharaoh had a dream (Genesis 41:1). However, sometimes the distinctions are not so easily drawn.

Many commentators class the stories of Abraham, Isaac and Jacob as folk tales rather than history. Some Jewish rabbis classified the story of Jonah as a parable. However, in these cases, there is no textual reason to think of them as anything other than history. They describe historical places and use historical names for people. They set the events within the flow of biblical history. They draw on relevant features of life at the time in which they are set. So why not treat the stories of Abraham or Jonah as historical? The major reason is the presence of astounding miracles. A fish that can swallow a man for three days, for example? However, this is really beside the point. If we believe in a God who created the universe and can influence that universe at will, then we have grounds to believe in the possibility of miracles. After all, nothing is too difficult for God (Genesis 18:14). The presence of a miracle cannot in itself be enough to rule that a story is not history.

God chose to use the story form to reveal himself, presumably because it is a good way to convey not only historical events, but also their meaning, in a way we could appreciate. Stories are easier to follow than arguments. We identify with the characters and their experiences. A story engages our emotions and feelings. In a good story, we care about the characters. Stories are more memorable than their lessons. Long after we have forgotten the point of a sermon we once heard, we will still remember a story the preacher told.

So describing biblical history as consisting of stories does not mean that we are dismissing their historical value. In fact, the story form is an ideal way of conveying the theological significance of historical events. One evangelical theologian notes, 'It is the greater interpretative (explanatory) capacity of literary narrative over bare chronicle that makes it the preferred medium of biblical historiography.'[3] A story can tell you why something happened and how people felt. Far from being a handicap to history, the story form can help us really grasp what actually happened in a way that the bare statement of facts does not.

The way they told them

But the stories of the Old Testament also reflect peculiar features of Hebrew storytelling. Even when recording historical events, they are recorded in cultural forms that sound like a good yarn. This does not mean they are not true, only that they are told in the traditional form of storytelling. If we really want to understand these stories and see the world from within them, then we will need to understand these conventions.

Some of these conventions are not unique to the ancient Hebrews, but simply part of what makes a good story in any time or place. Many people are great storytellers, fluent in the art, and don't even realize it. They may tell us something historical that really happened, but they will do so as if they were telling us a story. There is a beginning, a middle and an end to their tale. Regardless of whether we travel back in time three thousand or thirty years, we will find that some features of stories are universal. In general, a story follows a linear progressive plot. Even when a modern film or novel plays with flashbacks, we will reconstruct in our minds the linear story we are being told.

A selection process

Good storytellers are selective in their material. We have all had the experience of listening to someone tell us about a trip to the doctor's office and leaving nothing out. We hear all about the bus route, who was on the bus, what the doctor was wearing, and all the gory details of their physical ailments. Such people may be good talkers, but not necessarily good storytellers. They overload their story with so much information that you lose the thread, grow restless and just want them to get to the point and finish. You recoil at the private medical information they divulge and really would prefer not to know so much detail! By not being selective enough, this person is spoiling their story.

Being selective means drawing our attention to what matters and not distracting people with too many fussy details. Indeed, sometimes a story works well because of what is *not* said. Particularly if we want to teach a moral lesson, we can do better to tell a story with an obvious inference, rather than point out the moral. To take an example, think of what the book of Esther leaves out: in fact, it's the only book in the Bible that does not mention God![4]

So does God make no appearance in Esther? A first reading suggests so. Events just happen, and characters do what they can. God seems notable by his absence. But the events betray a high degree of unlikely coincidence. There happened to be a Jew in the court of the Persian king, and he happened to have a beautiful adoptive daughter, Esther, who attracts the king's favour and becomes his favourite queen. Esther happens to be a Jewish queen in the court of Persia (Esther 2:17). What follows is a series of coincidences at a time of national crisis. The entire Israelite people in Persia face genocide, the plot is uncovered, and Esther is in just the right place at just the right time to protect her people. In many ways, it all comes down to the position and wisdom of another Jew, Mordecai (Esther 10:3). However, that is hardly the lesson we should learn from the story. Who put Mordecai in that position? Who gave Esther her beauty? Who ensured that conversations were overheard, plots unravelled and wicked individuals found out? We are supposed to fill in the gaps and identify God as the hidden presence through the unfolding story. Here is a good lesson for us to learn from the book of Esther, because it is also a lesson we need to learn about our own lives!

Reading the clues

Hebrew narratives are generally short and simple, and do not tell us everything we might want to know. Indeed, entire books can be written, speculating about information that the Bible does not actually give us. But the brevity and simplicity are because the Israelites were fine storytellers, knowing all too well how to select and craft their historical material into a form that would make a good, memorable and thought-provoking read. Old Testament Bible scholar Dale Ralph Davis has provided a helpful survey of many features found in Hebrew narrative. He reminds us that 'Biblical writers did not have the luxury of using bold, italicized, or underlined type, as our computer-driven generation does. They had to make their emphases in different ways.'[5] Spotting these story features helps us to grasp their meaning and read them in the way they were intended.

Silences that speak

The first feature we should be aware of is the economy of Hebrew vocabulary. This is one danger in our English translations. Many contemporary versions use a variety of words to translate the same Hebrew word. They do so in order to bring out the meaning of a phrase in terms a modern English speaker can understand. But this can also obscure the simplicity of the underlying narrative. Hebrew stories can be sparse and yet effective. Sometimes the Hebrew writings seem deliberately to avoid telling us information we feel we need to know.

In English stories, we are used to having many descriptive details, simply because they help our imagination. We like to know a door was wooden, a beard was long or a car was silver.

There may not be any significance in these details, but they do bring a story to life. Because Hebrew narrative tends to be fairly simple, descriptive detail stands out. Why are we told, for example, that Esau is a 'hairy man' (Genesis 27:11)? Because it will be important later in the story when his brother wears a goatskin in order to impersonate him. Why do we need to know that Ehud was 'left-handed' (Judges 3:15)? Because this unusual characteristic would enable him to hide his sword and assassinate the king of Moab. Rather than simply reading these details as aids to making the story come alive, they are important to the plot. As we read Hebrew stories, we should be alert to details. They are often there for a reason.

What *were* they thinking?

Another stark difference between a modern novel and an Old Testament story is the relative lack of interior monologue. When the student ran from the lecture room, she thought to herself, 'I can still catch the bus and make the evening show!' Such an interior monologue is useful. We get to see inside a character's mind and understand her motivation or feelings. But the Bible writers only rarely use this device. (Good examples are Genesis 18:12; 1 Samuel 27:1; and 1 Kings 12:26.) However, the Hebrew writers gave clues to the interior thoughts of their characters by other means.

One moving example of this is found in Genesis 22, the story of Abraham taking his son Isaac to Mount Moriah. God had called upon him to offer Isaac as a sacrifice, and Abraham obediently set out. What was he thinking? How did he feel? You cannot read the narrative and imagine that this was cold obedience. Notice how God identifies the sacrificial victim: 'Take your son, your only son, whom you love—Isaac' (Genesis 22:2). He need only have said, 'Take Isaac', but the four different ways of describing Isaac emphasize what he meant to his father: a son, an only son, a beloved son, a son he had named after the laughter that accompanied Isaac's birth in old age. Now how do you think Abraham was feeling?

Slowly the story unfolds, with details like the wood being cut, and the donkey and servants who accompanied them. Tension builds as they approach the place of sacrifice. Notice how Isaac raises his question: 'Isaac spoke up and said to his father Abraham, "Father?" "Yes, my son?" Abraham replied' (Genesis 22:7). When stories tend to be told in as few words as possible, we must ask why these words are actually there. Why not just get to the point? Our attention is drawn to the relationship of father and son that is about to be put to the ultimate test. And what happens when Abraham finally reaches the point of sacrifice? 'Then he reached out his hand and took the knife to slay his son' (Genesis 22:10). Again, notice how unnecessary this sentence is as far as mere information is concerned. Why do we need to know that he 'reached out his hand'? Surely we already know that he takes his knife in order 'to slay his son'? The slow, tense, detailed narrative helps us to be participants in the story. Without any interior monologue, we can feel the depth, pain, mystery and misery of the moment.

Of course, there are other clues that remind us of Abraham's faith in a God who would never tolerate human sacrifice. As he heads off up the mountain with his son, he tells his servants, 'We will worship and then we will come back to you' (Genesis 22:5). To his son, Abraham says, 'God himself will provide the lamb' (Genesis 22:8). Abraham was sure that somehow this would not be the end of the story for Isaac. But even this man of faith who reasoned that he could trust God (Hebrews 11:17–19) must have experienced deep anguish and confusion as he made the way to Moriah. The story is told in a way that makes us feel this too.

Warts and all

Early history took the form of propaganda. From Egypt and Babylon, we have examples of this. This kind of writing recorded victories, successes and achievements. If you were a king, the last thing you would want recorded were your failures or defeats. But the Old Testament stories are not propaganda, something we see clearly in the way the weaknesses of its characters are on display.

Abraham was a liar and slept with his mistress. Sarah laughed at God's promise and even tried to lie to God. Isaac was a deceiver who was himself deceived by his son Jacob. Jacob becomes one of the great tricksters of the Bible, deceiving all and sundry. After a wrestling match with God, he receives a new nickname. 'Israel' means 'struggles with God', and Israel becomes not only a new name for Jacob, but the name of God's chosen people—those who struggle with God. Joseph, the dreamer who provides salvation for God's people in a time of famine, was also Joseph the arrogant, spoilt younger child of Jacob. And all of these examples come within the first of the Old Testament's thirty-nine books! We have not even mentioned the failings and weaknesses of God's judges and kings—and those make a long list indeed! Old Testament narrative demonstrates a brutal honesty. Undoubtedly, the truth about human nature is far more important than the presentation of a whitewashed history.

Not telling

So the Hebrew writers did not record everything we might want to know. And their selectivity can be instructive. For often we need to think about what we are not being told, in order to realize what we *are* being told!

Take the ending of Jonah. Don't you want to know what happened to him? Why leave the story with him being admonished by God for his grumpiness? Don't you want a little 'happily-ever-after' paragraph to show what Jonah did next? The Bible does not give it. Why? Because the book of Jonah is not about Jonah. It is about God and God's relationship to humanity. We learn more about God in his grace here than we do about Jonah in his grouch! To have filled in the gaps in our knowledge of Jonah would have satisfied our curiosity but distracted our theology.

In 2 Samuel 6 we read that David brought the ark of the covenant from Kiriath Jearim to Jerusalem, the new capital. All was going well, with priests guiding the cart and musicians providing a marching band, until an ox stumbled, Uzzah reached out his hand to steady the ark, and God struck Uzzah dead. The musicians stopped playing, David got scared, and the ark was hastily hidden away in a nearby house. The passage doesn't tell us why Uzzah died, other than indicating he had been 'irreverent' (verse 7). But, we wonder, what is so irreverent about steadying the ark as an ox stumbles and it slips from the cart?

The answer is found in what the passage does not tell us. We know elsewhere that the ark was never supposed to be transported with the use of animals, but only by particular people (Exodus 25:12–14). We also learn that the ark itself was not to be touched (Numbers 4:15)—it was to be carried by people using poles. So the story of Uzzah describes people taking the things of God for granted—the law has been neglected and priests are being careless in worship. Having grown up with the ark in his family home (2 Samuel 6:3), Uzzah was no longer in awe of it, and his action in steadying the ark actually revealed his casual attitude to God. In the words of a modern maxim: 'Familiarity breeds contempt.'

Selectivity makes us stop and read a passage again. What did we miss? What are we not being told? As Davis writes, 'They probably want us to think about their stories. Why should they always spoon-feed us?'[6]

A funny thing happened

It's often said that sarcasm is the lowest form of wit. But satire uses sarcasm to great effect, drawing attention to people's stupidity. Sarcasm often involves a striking and humorous contrast. I think the Bible finds many things funny, and indeed God laughs too (Psalm 2:4).

A great example is found in Elijah's confrontation with the prophets of Baal on Mount Carmel. During a drought, the challenge is for them to call out to Baal to answer their requests, just as Elijah will then call out to the Lord. The prophets of Baal receive no answer, despite their noise, activity and self-mutilation. Elijah says, 'Shout louder! . . . Surely he is a god! Perhaps he is deep in thought, or busy, or travelling. Maybe he is sleeping and must be awakened' (1 Kings 18:27). The New Living Translation of the same passage lays it on thick: '"You'll have to shout louder," he scoffed, "for surely he is a god! Perhaps he is daydreaming, or is relieving himself. Or maybe he is away on a trip, or is asleep and needs to be wakened!"'[7]

Sometimes the sarcasm will make a pointed remark about someone's behaviour. This is important, because Hebrew narratives only rarely make overt judgments about the behaviour of their subjects. We have to read between the lines to notice what is wrong. In the story of David and Bathsheba, we are confronted by David's sin in committing adultery, but the story begins with a simple reference to the time of year: 'In the spring, at the time when kings go off to war . . . David remained in Jerusalem' (2 Samuel 11:1). The writer does not tell us directly, but we are to notice that King David is neglecting his duty as king leading his men in battle. This is the start of a downward moral spiral. And what of Bathsheba? Is she so pure? Why then is she bathing in a place where David can see her from his rooftop? When she sleeps with the king, we are also told that she has taken the trouble to purify herself in accordance with the law (2 Samuel 11:4). Perhaps there is a touch of sarcasm here too the woman who keeps her legal observance is also able to get herself into bed with the king. What kind of hypocrisy is this?

I have no doubt that the Israelites laughed as they heard the story of Balaam and his donkey. Balaam is a pagan prophet from Moab. He is sent to curse the wandering Israelites as they make their way from Egypt to the Promised Land. But the donkey he is riding sees an angel of the Lord blocking their way and refuses to proceed. Three times this happens, and three times Balaam beats his donkey. Finally, the donkey speaks: 'What have I done to you to make you beat me these three times?' Rather than being taken by surprise, Balaam complains, 'You have made a fool of me!' and threatens it (Numbers 22:28–29). A clear contrast emerges. Balaam's donkey is a greater prophet than its master. It sees an angel that is invisible to the prophet. It speaks with sense, whereas the prophet speaks nonsense. Who, we now ask, is the real donkey in this passage?

Going on and on

If there is something that puts the modern reader off the Bible, it is repetition. Isn't repetition boring and tedious? Isn't repetition boring and tedious? But there is more going on than meets the eye. Of course, repetition may partly reflect an oral culture. Remember, most ancient Israelites had no access to the written scrolls of the books we are concerned with.[7] They would have known their contents through hearing them read and then repeating them aloud. But repetition is more than simply an aid for the memory.

Repetition can involve a lengthy passage or a frequently repeated key word or phrase. (Theologians call this a *leitwort*, which just means the same thing but sounds more clever.) The first chapter of Genesis repeats a number of words: day, good, heavens and earth, in a way that suggests the author clearly had rhythm. Susan Niditch observes, 'The repeated frames in Genesis 1 . . . create the impression of a magisterial and in-charge deity whose word is all-powerful, whose creations are firmly rooted, solid, and integrated.'[8] Repetition in this case sounds like the sequential orders of a powerful king. The very tone of the first chapter of Genesis implies that God is the King who rules by decree.

When the law provides instructions for the building of the tabernacle, it then seems tedious to read about the building of the tabernacle in almost the same words again. But that itself tells us something significant—the Israelites were being obedient in following God's plans. What God asked them to do, they did. To the letter. As the Old Testament unfolds, we find such obedience sadly unusual.

Some stories give us a sense of déjà vu. The story of Abram and Pharaoh (Genesis 12:10–20), Abraham and Abimelek (Genesis 20:1–18) and Isaac and Abimelek (Genesis 26:1–16) are all remarkably similar. They all tell of a patriarch escaping famine by fleeing to a foreign land where he has to pretend his wife is his sister in order to protect himself. The outcome of each story is much the same. Similar stories suggest to some commentators that the writers have been confused.

One original event has been retold in different ways, and the incorporation of more than one variation on the same story indicates sloppy editing. However, there are better ways of understanding these similar stories.

First, repeated events suggest certain patterns in history. Sadly, people don't really change. 'What goes around comes around,' we sometimes say. Secondly, repetition reflects genre. Robert Alter suggests that he came to recognize this when thinking about television westerns. I have never really been a fan of westerns. And because I rarely watch them, I imagine they are all similar—saloon doors swinging, sheriff badge flashing, guns shooting. Of course, if you are a fan of the western movie, you will be offended. You will be able to point out just how different they all are. The genre makes the story look repetitive, but if you are an enthusiast, each film offers a unique story.

Repeated phrases should also catch our attention. These are the equivalent of a highlighter pen or underlining. While the stories of the judges, like Gideon and Samson, are all quite different, they are written in similar ways and use similar phrases. Repetitive phrases (Judges 3:7, 12; 4:1; 6:1) suggest that history is repeating itself. The Israelites 'did evil in the eyes of the Lord'; the Lord 'sold them' or 'gave them' into the hands of their enemies. Then the people 'cried out to the Lord' and he provided a judge to deliver them. After a period of peace, the cycle repeats itself.

What is the problem with these people? Why do they keep returning to their idolatry, and why does history keep repeating itself? Another repeated phrase in the book of Judges supplies the answer: 'In those days Israel had no king; everyone did as they saw fit' (Judges 17:6; 18:1; 19:1; 21:25). Repetition in the book of Judges prepares us for the sending of a king in the books that follow.

Watch out for the chiasm

I held this term back until last because it may sound a little intimidating. Now we are touching on a more technical term in Hebrew literature.

A chiasm (pronounced kiy-asm) is a literary construction that helps to highlight a point. It involves presenting the main point of your story in an appetizing way. Think of the best way to eat a slice of ham. You could eat it straight out of the packet, but a nicer way would be between two slices of bread. A whole lot more appetizing, in fact! The slices of bread are symmetrical; the slice of ham is unique.

When a story is written in the form of a chiasm, it means that the main point of the story will be found somewhere in its centre. The narrative on either side of the main point will be parallel.

'Chiasm' is a Greek word meaning 'cross'. Think of it as an 'X' that marks the spot. If a story is written in the form of a chiasm, it means your attention will be drawn to an X marking the central phrase or statement. Chiasms are not unique to Hebrew literature. In English literature, they can be found in Chaucer, Milton and Shakespeare. But the Israelites were particularly fond of the chiasm, and you will find examples among the psalms and the law, as well as in the narratives.

A good example of a chiasm is found in the account of the Genesis flood. The structure is very detailed, but we may notice something is going on, simply by observing the duration of various events. Twice we are told that seven days are spent waiting for the flood (7:4, 10), and twice we are told that seven days are spent waiting for the waters to subside (8:10, 12). The rain falls for forty days (7:17), and forty days also mark a wait at the end of the flood (8:6). The waters cover the land for 150 days (7:24), and the waters recede over 150 days (8:3). When we lay these numbers out in a sequence, a pattern becomes clear: 7, 7, 40, 150, 150, 40, 7, 7. There is a symmetry between these two halves. This focuses our attention on a central statement: 'God remembered Noah' (Genesis 8:1). This statement will be key to unlocking the meaning of the story. Though a judgment has fallen through the great flood, God has made a covenant with Noah and will honour that covenant promise. The act of remembering, when applied to God, does not suggest that God was suffering from a bad memory. Remembering implies bringing to mind a promise that God will act upon in deliverance (Genesis 19:29). Any hope in the story will be found in the faithfulness of God, and, we learn, God is faithful and delivers on his promise.[9] None of this discussion indicates that the flood did not happen the way in which we have read it, nor should we think the numbers are merely symbolic. But the writer has taken time to structure his material in a very carefully ordered manner.

When students of the Bible first come across the idea of a chiasm, they often greet it with suspicion. Doesn't it sound a bit artificial and contrived? It's worth remembering that the stories in the Bible were carefully written: writers did not just ramble, but chose their words carefully. It is probably better to describe many of these stories as 'literary history' rather than 'literal history', not because the events did not happen, but because they have been carefully written using literary forms. It's also important to know that writing in the form of a chiasm probably came naturally to an Israelite. The chiasm is particularly appropriate for the flood: 'Noah enters the ark and later leaves it. The waters rise and then fall. In other words, the story falls naturally into two halves that ought to resemble each other to some extent. The surface structure of the narrative mirrors the deep structure of the event being described.'[10]

Entering the story

So when we listen to the stories of the Hebrew Bible, we are engaging with real history, but doing so through a way of writing that may seem alien to us. It is repetitive and aids memorization. It is economic in its use of words, and therefore each word should be assumed to have value. The stories may be humorous, even crude, and they are certainly honest in their descriptions. The accounts can be both historical and yet driven by a theological agenda. That agenda will be very important to us. As the Word of God, the Bible can be read not simply as a record of things that happened, but an explanation of why things happened. The stories fit into one grand story, called salvation history. This is the story of creation, human rebellion and God's rescue plan. Through the unfolding history of the Israelites, we are clearly shown the weakness of the human heart and the need for a superhuman deliverer.

These ancient stories point beyond themselves to the New Testament story of the incarnation. But before we reach ahead to our Christian understanding of Old Testament stories, let's take time to read them through ancient eyes. They make us think, make us laugh, and sometimes they confuse us. But they always help us see a new world in a new way. Through these stories, we can travel far back in time.

Bible field trip

Reading: Judges 3:12–30
Date: 1200 BC
Destination: Moab

1. How many descriptive details are given in this story that reveal Ehud's plan?

2. How is being left-handed a benefit to Ehud?

3. What transpires to make it possible for Ehud to escape?

4. Think of another story that shows how something that might be inconsequential, or even a handicap, becomes the means of victory.

3

ON LOCATION

The development of GPS navigation systems has led to an awful loss of common sense and instinct on the part of drivers the world over. Relying on satellite-based directions, rather than visual signs, landmarks and other clues, has led to many disastrous journeys. When a sixty-seven-year-old Belgian woman left home to pick up a friend from a railway station in her nearby city of Brussels, she set up her sat nav for the thirty-eight-mile drive by car. Something was wrong with the system, and, as reported by the *Daily Mail* in Great Britain, 900 miles later she arrived in the Croatian capital of Zagreb. Only then realizing her mistake, she turned around and drove back, arriving in Brussels two days late for her friend, by which time Belgian police had launched a manhunt. She said, 'I saw all kinds of traffic signs along the road. First in French, then in German: Köln, Aachen, Frankfurt. But I didn't ask myself any questions. I just kept accelerating.' How is it possible for someone to ignore all those signs? 'I was just distracted and preoccupied,' she said.

We too can be distracted and preoccupied as we read the Bible. We fail to notice the landscape, place names and geography. Perhaps it seems alien to us, so we ignore such details and read on, hoping to encounter some devotional verse that warms our hearts, even if we are clueless about what is going on elsewhere. But the Bible unfolds in time and place. History matters, as we locate ourselves in time and ask what year it might be. And geography matters too. These events happen in real places. Reading Scripture confronts us with place names, ancient empires and descriptions of hills, valleys, mountains and lakes, reminding us we are not only somewhere in history, but somewhere on planet Earth. We will now survey the location of Old Testament events and see how this helps us understand the text from the inside.

The big picture

A satellite image of the Middle East is a great one to use in order to get a sense of the wider perspective. You have the Mediterranean Sea on the left. (The Bible calls this the Great Sea.) Here the island of Cyprus stands out like a stingray, with its tail pointing north-east. The land mass above Cyprus is modern-day Turkey, or ancient Anatolia, the land of the Hittites. To the south of Cyprus lies the North African coastline. Of most importance for Bible history will be the land of Egypt. Here the green vegetation along the fertile Nile Valley stands out like a thread. The ancient Egyptian empire was spread along this narrow ribbon in the hostile desert. Notice how the green area spreads out as it reaches the sea. This is the Nile River Delta, where the waters fan out and allow for a much wider area of cultivated land. The land of Goshen lies in this region, where the Israelites lived and laboured as slaves.

Moving east of Egypt, we cross the Sinai Peninsula, flanked by two important fingers of water that stretch to the Red Sea and, from there, into the Arabian Sea and the Indian Ocean. The furthest of these gulfs is the modern-day Red Sea, but whether or not that was the Red Sea of the exodus is a matter of some controversy that we will consider later. In ancient times, either of these bodies of water could be called the Red Sea.

Following the coastline of the Mediterranean from Egypt, we come to the land of Canaan. You can trace a line from the Sinai Peninsula northwards through the Dead Sea, along the Jordan River, past the Sea of Galilee and on into Syria. This line roughly marks the eastern edge of what will become the land of Israel. To the east of this line notice how the land turns to a vast desert. Looking down from the skies during the night, areas of settlement will stand out, with their lights glowing, but the vast areas of sea and desert will remain inky black.

Heading north from Canaan, we encounter two great rivers (the Tigris and Euphrates) flowing from the high ground towards the south-east, emptying out in the Persian Gulf. The Euphrates marks a symbolic northern limit of the influence of Israel. It is called the 'great river' in the Bible (Joshua 1:1–4). Israel never really settled such a large territory. Along this important river valley, other great civilizations will rise and fall. The Sumerians, Assyrians and Babylonians will all owe their existence to the life sustained by these important rivers.

A large river is a life-support system to a land that is predominantly arid desert. Egyptian and Assyrian culture would both thrive on the Tigris, Euphrates, and Nile. A thousand miles separated these two great cultures, and so, in early history, their contact was naturally limited.

However, this wider area is known as the Fertile Crescent. Stretching from the mouth of the Tigris across to the Nile River, this is a somewhat crescent-shaped area of land, much more fertile than the adjoining deserts.

The land bridge

From this brief survey, something very important stands out. As we look at the position of Canaan, we are actually staring at a meeting point for three great continents. Europe, Africa and Asia all bump together (or pull apart!) at this particular point. In fact, the line from the Red Sea, through the Dead Sea, along the Jordan River looked uncannily straight, didn't it? It is actually a rift valley where two continents are moving. Sometimes called the 'Great Rift Valley', in its full extent it is really a system of rift valleys stretching for 3,700 miles from northern Syria into Mozambique in Africa. This geological feature explains the frequency of earthquakes in the region.

As a meeting point of continents, the little land of Canaan would have assumed an importance far beyond its physical size. It would always be a country punching far above its weight, forming, as it did, a land bridge for the continents. Trade travelling between Asia, Europe and Africa was likely to come through here. Think of the traders and armies moving about the ancient world. Regardless of their destination, there are two places to avoid—the sea and the desert. The sea is dangerous and, despite a few seafaring peoples (like the Phoenicians), generally risky for transporting large quantities of goods or people. Likewise, the desert is a great obstacle. With the domestication of the camel, trade routes opened up across the desert lands, but camels were clearly not an attractive option for moving much material or many soldiers. Therefore, all this travel becomes funnelled into the narrow little bridge we call the land of Canaan. It was through this land that Hittites from the north, Nubians from the south and Babylonians from the east would travel.

Land grab

The land of Canaan was not particularly important or rich in itself. But it was enormously strategic. So all the major empires of the Ancient Near East would lay claim to it as their own. Controlling Canaan would mean controlling the trade routes, and that meant taxes. It would also provide security for the great empires, as any large military movement would have to come this way.

But the effect of being funnelled through a narrow land bridge becomes even more remarkable when you look at the land up close. The major trade roads through Canaan are limited. Some of the country is difficult terrain, not lending itself to a swift north-south journey. Therefore, most movement will be channelled along particular roads. In the Bible, they are called the King's Highway (Numbers 20:17–19) and the Way of the Sea, also known as the Way of the Philistines (Exodus 13:17; NIV 'road through the Philistine country'). Therefore, most traders and soldiers of the ancient world would have to travel through certain valleys. One of those valleys, Jezreel, was dominated by the ancient city of Megiddo, and all those travelling the Way of Sea would pass through it. Controlling this one city meant control of the valley, and that was very important for exercising authority over the land bridge. Many battles in the ancient world, and even in more recent history, have been fought in this particular valley. In the ancient world, it was called Armageddon, after the hill of Megiddo, and the name has, of course, become a metaphor for a final, great conflict.

At any time in the ancient world, surveying the wider area, Israel would not have seemed like an important nation. In fact, much of the time, it was either a province of a greater empire, like Egypt or Babylon, or considered a rather lawless land. Cities in this region were often fortified and frequently fell victim to rival armies. But the land had a strategic value to all those great empires, and so it should not surprise us to read about biblical places and people in the texts and inscriptions of those greater powers. The land of Canaan has an importance beyond its size or resources, and continues to preoccupy political and military interests today.

Borders and boundaries

A little smaller than the state of Maryland, the region in which most Old Testament events took place was not enormous. The Bible provides a description of the geographical extent of the land (Genesis 10:19). But it is important to avoid reading a verse like this through modern eyes and imagine passport control or strictly agreed boundaries. The modern nation state did not actually exist in the ancient world. The nearest equivalent would be city states, which could form loose alliances. Until the arrival of the Israelites, many of the towns in Canaan probably considered themselves to be independent cities. So there was never a political nation called Canaan or a land with fixed borders.

When the Israelites arrived in the land, there was a clearer sense of the limits of their territory. You would have needed to pack a range of different clothes for the different climates you would encounter. The southern border would be the 'Desert of Zin' (Numbers 34:3), the edge of the desert area in which the Israelites wandered for forty years with Moses. More specifically, the 'Wadi of Egypt' provides a physical border, as rivers often provided this function in the ancient world (Numbers 34:5–6). The northern limit is part of a line running through Lebo Hamath (Numbers 34:8). No one is entirely sure if Lebo Hamath was a city or simply the border of a northern kingdom. The eastern edge of the land runs to the east of the Sea of Galilee and down the Jordan River Valley through the Dead Sea (Numbers 34:10–12).

The actual area where the Israelites settled, and which we might refer to as the land of Israel, is somewhat smaller. 'From Dan to Beersheba' (1 Kings 4:25), a distance of about 150 miles (240 km), refers to the real extent of the northern and southern borders of Israelite settlement at the time of its greatest security and peace under King Solomon. An overview of the land is provided for Moses from his vantage point on Mount Nebo, east of the Dead Sea (Deuteronomy 34:1–3). From here, Moses had an unparalleled view from Dan in the far north, the Mediterranean far to the west and down to the Negev desert in the south.

Hitting the holy road

Put on some decent walking boots, and we can cover most of the land quite comfortably. In the north lies the region of the city of Dan. This area was settled by the tribe of Naphtali and was very green and fertile. The most important source for the Jordan River would be the snows on Mount Hermon (9,230 ft high). There are other mountains in the area, but the summit of each can be reached without any special equipment or too much effort.

This region would become the Galilee of the New Testament. In Old Testament times, the Sea of Galilee was called the Sea of Kinnereth. Also called the Sea of Tiberias in the New Testament, it is more accurately described by Luke as a lake (Luke 8:22) rather than a sea. This large inland lake is not quite large enough to be a real sea, but could support a significant fishing industry. About 13 miles long and 8 miles wide, the lake covers a total area of 64 square miles. Many lakes in the United States are considerably larger. Lake Erie has a surface area one hundred times greater than Galilee. Even Lake Tahoe, on the California-Nevada border, is a little over double the size of Galilee. So this is a lake not large enough ever to lose sight of the shore, but large enough to be dangerous in a storm.

Along the edge of the Mediterranean Sea lies the coastal plain. In many ways, this is the most productive place to live. The land is flat and easy to travel through; it has access to the sea and is good for farming. Sounds like the best place to settle as an Israelite. But that wasn't how things worked out! A seafaring people called the Philistines arrived here from the Aegean and took control of much of this region. Another seafaring people, the Phoenicians, occupied the northern reaches, and so the Israelites never did have much opportunity to become a seafaring people themselves.

The central hill country of Israel would be where the Israelites really found their home. Rising up from the coastal plain, this system of hills and valleys provided good grazing for sheep, fertile valleys for farming and secure hill tops for defensive towns. One of the most important of these valleys was the Jezreel, with its important ancient town of Megiddo. Also, on a hill overlooking this valley was a very small, unimportant settlement that could have been forgotten to history: Nazareth. But it would grow in significance after the time of Jesus. Moving eastwards across the central hill country, the land rises to a peak and then descends quickly to the Jordan River Valley. The city of Jerusalem lies along this eastern limit of the central hills and mountains. That was why travellers would always have to ascend 'up' to Jerusalem or Mount Zion.

Rainwater from the Mediterranean falls across the land of Canaan, as clouds move eastward from the sea. But they don't reach the desert areas that drop down towards the Dead Sea. This region is sometimes called a 'pocket desert', but in the Bible, it is simply 'the wilderness'. Most of the waters arrive when it has been raining heavily in the west. This rain creates flash floods through the 'wadis' or gorges that run east through the desert. David will hide here during a rebellion, and Jesus will spend his time of temptation in this region. The wilderness is a place of refuge, contemplation and crime—the parable of the Good Samaritan concerns a violent robbery on a road down from Jerusalem through this pocket desert.

The Jordan River Valley marks another important geological feature in the land and provides suitable terrain for an important highway. However, its river was never as mighty as the Rivers Nile or Euphrates. In Egypt and across Mesopotamia, barges could travel up and down the major rivers, but the Jordan, being relatively shallow, did not lend itself to this kind of transportation. Indeed, you could have swum across or forded it at various points. During the time of Joshua, a miracle is required to stop the water and enable the Israelites to cross, but we are told that, at this time, the river was 'in flood' (Joshua 3:15).

Not all rivers run to the sea. The River Jordan makes its way southward, following the rift valley until it reaches the lowest point on earth. The name 'Jordan' is probably related to a Hebrew word meaning 'to go down', and it does indeed descend very rapidly—from the Sea of Galilee (695 ft [212 m] below sea level) to the Dead Sea (1300 ft [396 m] below sea level).[1] The Dead Sea, or Salt Sea in the Bible (Genesis 14:3), is sometimes called the Arabah, a reference to the region (Deuteronomy 3:17). As we know, this geological feature takes a position of honour in global geology. Because water cannot flow out of the Dead Sea, nothing leaves except through evaporation. And as water evaporates, the sea that remains increases in salt content. No life can survive in such salty water—no fish, no plants, no people, just a few simple bacteria. The sea is quite large, but only of use for minerals. But the region is not entirely inhospitable to life. North of the Dead Sea lies the oasis town of Jericho, the oldest continuously occupied city on earth. Other evidence of human settlement includes the remains of the Jewish fortress of Masada over-looking the Dead Sea, and the alternative Jewish community of Qumran whose hidden library of important Hebrew books became known as the Dead Sea Scrolls. On the eastern edge of the Dead Sea lie a number of mysterious Bronze Age city ruins, which some scholars believe are the Cities of the Plain mentioned in Genesis, including Sodom and Gomorrah. Archaeologist Steven Collins has recently made a convincing claim to have discovered the lost city of Sodom, north-east of the Dead Sea at Tall el-Hammam. One key to this exciting discovery was the geographical information provided within the Bible text. Abraham and Lot could see Sodom from the hills of Bethel and Ai, eastwards, across the plain of the River Jordan. The extensive Bronze Age ruins of a city within this line of sight fit descriptions of Sodom remarkably well.[2]

Beersheba, in the southern end of the land, was surrounded by dry desert. Water was harder to locate here, so wells became significant, and important towns needed cisterns to hold water for the dry season. Travelling without water would be deadly. Most walking would have been done during the night or early-morning hours, before the sun rose too high and temperatures soared.

Human remains

It is remarkable how much diversity such a small area of land can offer, and, given its strategic location between the continents, it should not surprise us that evidence from all eras of human settlement can be found throughout the country. When early human remains are being discussed, it is often East Africa that becomes the focus. But possibly some of the earliest remains of *Homo sapiens* can be found in the land of Canaan.

One of the oldest recognizable human skulls ever identified was discovered near the Sea of Galilee: *Homo sapiens* teeth found near Tel Aviv in 2006 are twice as old as the earliest African discoveries. Excavations at Jericho uncovered remains of the earliest farming community. Maybe one day, with more evidence, we may find the *Out of Africa* scenario being replaced by an *Out of Canaan!*[3]

The passing year

In more northern climates, we tend to mark the year by four seasons, but in Canaan there would have been only two: 'seedtime' and 'harvest' (Genesis 8:22). It was divided into twelve months, marked by the phases of the moon.

Somewhat confusingly, there are two different new years in the Jewish calendar. The New Year for counting the passing of the years is in Tishri/September. However, there is a different New Year for counting the reigns of kings and used for religious purposes. This New Year begins in a month called Nisan (though this was not a word used until late in the biblical period) around March/April, which marks the beginning of the harvests, starting with the barley harvest.

After Nisan, there was a period of successive harvests, as different crops came to their fruition at different times. The last harvest was that of olives, and the harvest season ended with the Festival of Tabernacles in September/October time, in the month called Tishri. Now begins the second season, which is the time for planting, the rainy season. So we have seedtime and harvest.

There were normally three periods of rain during the seedtime season. An early rain period was generally only light, helping to break up the soil for ploughing. Most would fall during a second period between December and February. The high ground could also see snowfall. And a 'latter rain' would fall around the time of the Hebrew New Year. This could be a blessing to aid growth (Deuteronomy 11:14; Zechariah 10:1) or, if a little too late, a disaster for the crops (1 Samuel 12:17).

Understanding the climate was a matter of life and death. Planting and harvesting had to take place at the right time, in order to ensure enough crops to survive. Knowing the phases of the moon and the movement of the constellations was crucial to knowing where in the year one was. Genesis emphasizes that this is why God placed the lights in the night sky (Genesis 1:14): the stars would be a free clock, always accurate and never needing winding up.

The Pleiades, with its brightest star, Alcyone, was an important marker in the sky for the ancient Israelites (Job 9:9).

Notice the significance of the constellations in the Old Testament. They are not important for astrological purposes, as if dictating our fate, but for marking the seasons. God 'made the Pleiades and Orion' (Amos 5:8), because the first constellation was dominant in the winter period (seedtime) and the second dominant in the summer (harvest).

A land of milk and honey

Much of Canaan would be good for some form of farming: crops of grain, olives, figs and grapes have always been particularly important. The 'honey' referred to in the Bible may refer to the sweet syrup produced from dates, rather than the honey of bees, which were less common (Judges 14:8). Herding sheep, goats and cows formed an important part of life, because all of these creatures provided the milk for which the land would be known. The settled farming communities also used oxen, particularly for ploughing, and donkeys for transportation. Horses and camels were more valuable creatures and not part of ordinary community life. The horse was used primarily by the military, and camels were used for the long-distance transportation of goods in difficult open countryside and journeys between cities and nations. This fact probably explains the lack of archaeological evidence for the early use of the camel, given that archaeologists tend to focus on settlements. Donkeys were used in the urban environment, and their remains have been found in these settings.

Walk on the wild side

Away from the villages and cities, Canaan provided a genuine wilderness refuge for all kinds of wild animals. The rock badger and ibex are common sights even today in the wilderness regions of Israel.

Snakes, scorpions, bears, antelopes, lions and wolves are all referred to in Scripture. But references to the hippopotamus, crocodile and monkey probably refer to creatures not native to the land. If you read the older King James Version of the Bible, you may be surprised to come across 'unicorns' (Psalm 22:21), but this is probably a reference to wild oxen, or the aurochs, which were the parents of domestic cattle and are now extinct. They would certainly have been a frightening sight out in the wild.

Other dangerous creatures include bears and lions. Canaan's bears were a form of brown bear living in the north of the land and farther into the mountains of Lebanon. The lion would have been dangerous to encounter, though we know that Samson and David were able to kill them (Judges 14:5–6; 1 Samuel 17:34–36). These are not references to the large African lion that we often imagine. The Asiatic lion, native to Canaan, is extinct in the wild and considerably smaller than the African cousin. It was formidable and dangerous, but an animal that an armed Israelite could hope to overcome successfully if attacked.

Another dangerous wild animal frequently referred to in the Bible is the dog. In Western Europe and America, we probably

Left: the rock badger inhabits the remote, rocky regions. This wise little mammal spends most of its life basking in the sun (Proverbs 30:26). Right: grooved hooves allow the mountain goat (ibex) to climb difficult crags (Psalm 104:18). The Israelites used its horns as trumpets.

always assume 'man's best friend' when we hear the word 'dog'. This was not the case for the Israelites, however. Dogs were wild, dangerous pack animals, scavenging on the fringes of the human settlement. *Dog* was a term of reproach, and even today across the Middle East, the dog does not have quite the honour and respect afforded it in the West. So dogs return to their vomit (Proverbs 26:11), and lap the blood of the dead (1 Kings 22:29–38). It's better to be a live dog than a dead lion, but that isn't really saying much (Ecclesiastes 9:4)!

Birds make frequent appearances in the pages of the Old Testament. The geographical significance of the land bridge was not only key to military generals and tax collectors, but also important to birds on their migratory paths. Even today, Galilee remains an area in which birds are channelled during their migrations between the northern and southern hemispheres. The fields, lakes and woods are preferable to the desert and sea on either side of the land bridge. Among the many birds ancient Israelites observed were hawks, buzzards, cranes, eagles, owls and ravens. Yet we should not read the Bible as a textbook on ornithology, because there is no careful taxonomy of these creatures. For example, the Hebrew term 'eagle' could refer to a number of different birds of prey, or even to the vulture, soaring high above the sun-scorched valleys.

However, more terrifying still than vulture, lion or snake must surely have been one of the most dangerous creatures of all: the locust. It may be small, but its eating habits make it a lethal visitor. A locust is a stage in the life of a particular type of grasshopper. During this stage, locusts migrate in swarms, travelling at the speed of the wind. This swarm is able to consume every crop in its path. The largest recorded swarm comprised 40 billion locusts covering a region of 400 square miles. And a massive swarm of locusts would be a disaster, spelling death to entire communities (Nahum 3:15–16).

Living on the land

Life in the land flowing with goat milk and date honey would be productive, but not easy. It would involve hard work and a close relationship to the land. The Israelites were in touch with the earth they farmed and with the changing seasons. Even those living in urban city environments remained in close proximity to the land and its crops and animals. We will meet Saul, the first properly appointed king of Israel, out ploughing in the field with his oxen when not on official duties (1 Samuel 11:5). To enter the world of ancient Israel is to return to the land. All our senses should be engaged, as we taste the sweet honey, smell the oxen, hear the cry of the buzzards, feel the longed-for rain on dry ground and see people hard at work, making this land their home.

Bible field trip

Reading: 1 Samuel 24:1–22
Date: 1020 BC
Destination: The desert in the Dead Sea region

1. Where does David choose to hide?

2. What advice do David's companions give him?

3. What does David prove by his actions?

4. Who is really in control in this episode?

4

GOING BACK TO OUR ROOTS

Who am I? Where did I come from? These are fundamental questions that most of us ask. This drives many of us, especially in later years, to research our genealogies. Sometimes this causes us to discover things about our past that we would rather not have known! A woman commissioned an author to research and write a book about her family tree. She was hoping it might reinforce her social status, but she was horrified to learn that one of her grandfathers had been electrocuted as a criminal in a New York prison. She wanted the information left out, but compromised with the author who agreed to mask the truth with the following description: 'One of her grandfathers occupied the chair of applied electricity at one of America's best-known institutions. He was very much attached to his position and literally died in the harness.' Be careful of searching out your past; you don't know what you might find!

The Bible is a book of origins. It follows a family tree from the very beginning to the time of Jesus. The book of Genesis is named after its first word, meaning 'beginning'. It tells us of the beginning of creation, the beginning of space and time, and the beginning of human life. One phrase that recurs throughout the first book of the Bible is often tranlsated, 'These are the generations' (NIV 'This is the account of'; Hebrew *toledoth*), and it could also be rendered, 'This is the family tree' (2:4; 5:1; 6:9; 10:1; 11:10; 11:27; 25:12; 25:19; 36:1; 37:2).[1] Genesis describes the genealogies both of creation and particular human lives. Why do we need these family trees? Because in them we will find our roots too.

Of myth and men

The original *Star Wars* movie opened with the lines: 'A long time ago, in a galaxy far, far away . . .' Director George Lucas was deliberately echoing the language of fairy tale: 'Once upon a time, in a land far away . . .' When we hear such words, we know that we are in the world of fairy tale. But when we turn to the Bible, instead of, 'Once upon a time . . .' we read, 'In the beginning . . .' (Genesis 1:1). Those words prime us to the fact that we are reading something historical. The genealogies or family trees scattered throughout Genesis remind us that, through the generations, we can trace a line from later history all the way back to our origins. Jesus, David, Abraham, Noah and Adam are all related, as Luke will later point out in his Gospel (Luke 3:23–38).

But could the opening chapters of Genesis be mythological? 'Myth' is a very loaded word, as we have seen already. Its meaning among scholars is not quite the same as the way the word is used in popular culture. Generally, when a story or idea is described as a myth, we take it to mean that it is not true.

Our English word 'myth' is directly borrowed from a Greek word: *mythos*, used to describe fiction. Thucydides, an early

Greek historian, distinguished his own attempt to write truthful history from what he called 'silly fables' (*mythos*).[2] In the New Testament, Paul is equally concerned to distinguish the gospel from myths (1 Timothy 1:4; 4:7). Peter distances his eyewitness record of history from invented myths (2 Peter 1:16). When someone describes Genesis as a collection of myths, it is hard to avoid the conclusion that what they mean is that it is a collection of fanciful fables.

Before C. S. Lewis became a Christian, he was troubled by the parallels between the gospel account of Jesus and ancient myths of a dying and rising redeemer God. However, part of his conversion was a realization that the gospel embodied important themes of ancient myth, while also being rooted in real historical times and places. In his words,

> The heart of Christianity is a myth which is also a fact. The old myth of the Dying God, *without ceasing to be myth*, comes down from the heaven of legend and imagination to the earth of history. It *happens*—at a particular place, followed by definable historical consequences.[3]

As Lewis responded to the Gospels, perhaps we should be willing to respond to Genesis. Here is an early record of creation that can be historical and yet also reflect timeless themes of human longing, anxiety and hope. Of course, a history of creation itself and early human development, in a matter of a few chapters, is bound to look different from a contemporary scientific textbook. We have already considered how Hebrew language is limited, technical terms are not available, and history is recorded using certain literary techniques. K. A. Kitchen, a scholar of ancient Egyptian and biblical history, describes the opening chapters of Genesis as 'protohistory'; others prefer 'prehistory'. Genesis is a compressed and accessible account of complex and grand themes from our earliest history.

History sheds light on the ancient past. It reveals to us things that we do not otherwise know. An important argument among Christians concerns the relationship between Genesis and modern science. The date of creation, the process of evolution, the extent of the flood all generate difficulties for those who want to harmonize their reading of the Bible with science. So how does Genesis shed light on contemporary science and secular history?

I think light provides a useful analogy to guide our journey. Think of the difference between a flashlight beam and a flood-light. When a large floodlight is switched on, perhaps at a concert, it will flood a stage with light. Everything is lit up. When a flashlight is switched on, it sends a narrow but bright beam of light to a fixed point. Both lights are useful in different contexts. If you are looking for something, a floodlight can be misleading. It lights up too much and overwhelms us with information. A flashlight can be useful to find something in the dark, lighting up a single area and revealing enough for us to take in. So is the light of Genesis more like a floodlight or a flashlight beam?

Christians will take different views. Some will hold that it is a floodlight, lighting up everything we want to know about the ancient world. It provides a date for creation, an explanation for the migration of peoples and all the processes involved in forming the present world. Others will hold that Genesis is more like the focused beam of a flashlight. It highlights what we need to know, but not everything we might *want* to know. It reveals all the things we need to understand about God's purposes and plan in salvation history. It does not reveal everything we might *want* to know. Taking this analogy further, we can explore Genesis as the beam of light revealing what we need to know about our origins and ancient past, but be cautious not to expect it to answer all the questions we might have.[4]

How it all began

Time travel can be a dangerous business. If we arrive too early, then maybe there will be no earth at all, or perhaps only fire or water. And you don't even want to think about landing among dinosaurs! So we want to know the date of creation, to know how far back in time we can travel.

When Archbishop James Ussher (1581–1656) added up the dates given in the Genesis genealogies, he arrived at 23 October 4004 BC, not far off the traditional date of 3761 BC given to creation by Jewish rabbinical traditions. However, there has always been a question mark over whether this is the correct way of reading Genesis. Augustine (354–430), the early-church theologian, wrote a detailed work on the interpretation of Genesis that gave this warning:

> There is a knowledge to be had, after all, about the earth, about the sky, about the other elements of this world, about the movements and revolutions or even the magnitude and distances of the constellations, about the predictable eclipses of moon and sun, about the cycles of years and seasons, about the nature of animals, fruits, stones and everything else of this kind. And it frequently happens that even non-Christians will have knowledge of this sort in a way that they can substantiate with scientific arguments or experiments. Now it is quite disgraceful and disastrous . . . that they should ever hear Christians spouting what they claim our Christian literature has to say on these topics, and talking such nonsense that they can scarcely contain their laughter

when they see them to be *toto caelo*, as the saying goes, wide of the mark.[5]

The book of Genesis tells us what we need to know about our ancient past, but not everything we might want to know. When discussing the age of the earth or the processes involved in creation, we should show respect for mainstream scientific thought, even in areas where we may be sceptical of its findings.

The Genesis record

The simple problem with finding the date of creation is that the narrative of the first eleven chapters of Genesis is highly compressed. Francis Schaeffer, a theologian who held a very high view of the authority of Scripture, also acknowledged the difficulty of dating creation from the early chapters of Genesis:

> Prior to the time of Abraham, there is no possible way to date the history of what we find in Scripture. . . . When the Bible itself reaches back and picks up events and genealogies in the time before Abraham, it never uses these genealogies as a chronology.[6]

Among Christians, there has never been agreement over how long the events of the first chapters of Genesis take place. Nowhere is this more complex and controversial than the opening chapter of Genesis. One reason for the controversy is that the universe appears to be very old. Given the speed of light and the distance of stars and galaxies from our earth, light itself suggests a universe very ancient indeed. Geology assumes that processes like erosion have occurred in the past at the same kind of rate as we observe them today. Given this assumption, rivers and mountains all seem to indicate an ancient earth. Scripture itself speaks of an earth that seems ancient (Genesis 49:26; Deuteronomy 33:15; Psalm 90:2–4). Of course, 'ancient' is a relative term, and you might say you have an aunt who is ancient, without intending to imply that she was born millions of years ago! But Scriptures like these do express our sense that the mountains have been around a long, long time rather than only having formed at the time of the flood.[7]

Whatever opinion we hold on the various theories concerning creation, a key to Genesis is that it describes origins from a perspective that makes sense to us. It does not describe creation from the point of view of a being living in another galaxy, or from the point of view of an armadillo. It does not even describe it from the point of view of someone living at that time, such as Adam. It describes creation from the point of view of the Israelites, probably at the time of Moses.

Earth is the central concern from the second verse. Genesis simply does not explain the processes involved in producing the earth; it begins with our habitat already in view. Do the sun and moon only come into existence on day four? Again, this is not something we can be dogmatic about, given the language of perspective. The text tells us that God said, 'Let there be lights in the vault of the sky to separate the day from the night' (1:14). This tells us how these heavenly bodies will function in creation, not how long they may already have been in existence. It is also on day four that we read, 'He also made the stars' (1:16). The Hebrew word translated 'made' is not the same as the word 'create' used in verse 1. To make something need not mean that something previously not existing came into existence. It may mean rather that something took on a new purpose. God took stars and made them fit for the purpose of being lights, or markers in the sky as a celestial calendar. If a pupil is 'made' a head girl, for example, it does not mean that she did not previously exist, but only that she was made to serve in this new appointment. Old Testament scholar, John Walton, comments, 'The text does not address how or when the bodies originated; rather, the assignment of function is described in the text by the verb *asah*.'[8] But notice how much this reading of Genesis acknowledges the importance of our vantage point. The stars are not themselves seasonal markers but, because of how they appear from our perspective on Earth, they have this function for us.

A striking feature of the Genesis account of creation is an unusual use of the Hebrew word 'lights' to describe the sun and the moon. Common Hebrew words for the latter are, like English, related to the names for deities. Sun and moon were both worshipped by idolatrous Israelites (2 Kings 23:5–11). Moses goes out of his way to use a different word for them. The only other way he uses the Hebrew word 'lights' is to describe the candles that burned in the tabernacle. The heavenly bodies are not themselves divine, but have a function given by the Creator God in his plan for humankind. Perhaps the tabernacle is a recreation of the heavens and the earth. There are seven moving lights in the night sky: the sun, the moon and five visible planets. And there are seven lights burning on the menorah in the tabernacle. The tabernacle provided a model of God ruling the heavens and the earth.[9]

Many commentators, holding to a high view of the Bible as the infallible Word of God, understand Genesis to employ literary features like these.[10] Given that it is an account of creation designed to be understood and instructive to an ancient Israelite, it may not address all the distinct questions of physics or geology from a modern reader. But none of this implies that Genesis is not historical. These weighty words of

Scripture reveal to us our origins and the origin of the universe itself. The universe reflects God's creative decree, an orderly process, a divine plan. Adam stands at the head of the human race and a creation that was originally declared 'good' that has now gone wrong. Francis Schaeffer, while refusing to be dogmatic about the age of the earth or the processes involved in creation, nonetheless held that 'both the Old and New Testaments deliberately root themselves back into the early chapters of Genesis, insisting that they are a record of historical events'.[11] Genesis provides a simple, clear account of God's creation of all things in history, but not necessarily an account that answers all our scientific questions.

The Adam's family

Adam and Eve occupy a special place in the creation account. Indeed, the work of creation is described as the preparation of a place for them. They are uniquely made in God's image and given the unique task of stewarding creation (Genesis 1:26–28). What it means to be made in God's image is probably related to the task they are then given to do. God is the kingly Creator, sovereign over all creation. Now Adam and Eve are made as co-regents, to rule, under God's authority, the creation in which they have been placed. They will never create out of nothing, but they will 'rule' or govern this good creation.

So where did Adam and Eve come from? God is described as forming one from the 'dust' of the ground and the other from the organic matter of the first. It should be no surprise then that scientists describe us as being formed out of stardust. The carbon of stars is an essential element of life. Genesis is already making the connection between human beings and the stuff of the earth.

Adam and Eve are the original parents of the human family. As such, they must have lived some time in the Stone Age. Harmonizing this with the archaeological record is difficult. Genesis describes the first people as having ability in language (2:19), farming (4:2), music (4:21) and metalwork (4:22). The archaeological record describes such skills as emerging over time, and reaching this level of sophistication only by about 4000 BC. This fits with the idea of a relatively recent creation of Adam and Eve, in which case any hominids who lived prior to them were not truly human. Alternatively, Adam's family began with a level of sophistication in earlier times that was subsequently lost.

The idea of a single pair from whom all people can trace their ancestry is in dispute. Most secular scientists probably think the evidence points to some kind of 'polygenesis', meaning that there were many ancient hominids who played a part in our common ancestry. However, common ancestry remains entirely possible within a scientific framework. Adam and Eve provide a basis for the unity of humankind. We are all brothers and sisters in a global family created by God:

Neolithic stone tower at Jericho, ancient by the time of Joshua, one of the earliest stone constructions found anywhere in the world. Note modern steps on right of tower.

If we cannot insist on a common origin for all mankind, then we have given up the grounds, both from the Bible and common sense, for affirming the common dignity of all people, and their common need of the solution that the Biblical faith claims to offer. Therefore, abandoning our common origin looks like a dangerous mistake.[12]

All people on earth are descendants of a couple made in the image of God, with a particular dignity, purpose and destiny. But the Bible also reveals that something went wrong, as we saw earlier.

Adam and Eve are provided with a garden in a region called Eden. From the point of view of the Israelites, this was 'in the east' (Genesis 2:8). Given the geographical pointers, this places Eden somewhere in the region of the Tigris and Euphrates River Valley. Interestingly, this will be the general region from which Abraham will come.

The fall guy

A temptation arrived in the garden from outside, in the form of some kind of lizard. Ancient reliefs and seals from Mesopotamia often show the motif of a dragon-like creature. We call it a serpent, but at some point it may have had legs which were then lost (Genesis 3:14). From later biblical teaching, we know that this creature was Satan (Revelation 12:9), but Adam and Eve did not know this. Genesis merely hints that there was already a spiritual rebellion underway outside the garden, and the temptation was brought from there to Adam and Eve. (We have already met this couple in our first chapter. We will read more about this rebellion in chapter 6, but Genesis is silent on such wider cosmic issues.)

The first people were given a simple law to avoid eating the fruit from the tree of the knowledge of good and evil. In many ways, it does not matter much what this knowledge actually entailed. Whatever it was, it was something that only God could or should have. To 'know' in Hebrew means more than simply an abstract knowledge of the facts—it implies a more intimate relationship. Perhaps the knowledge of good and evil means the kind of relationship to good and evil that actually decides what those categories are. God's own nature determines what is good and evil. He is good, and what he is opposed to is evil. So, in that sense, God has knowledge of good and evil. By eating the fruit of this tree, Adam and Eve were taking matters into their own hands, throwing God's single, simple law into the dustbin and choosing to make up their own rules, rather than living under God's authority. That explains why God would declare, 'The man has now become like one of us, knowing good and evil' (Genesis 3:22).

So we must add to our description of every man and woman being made in the image of God the qualification that this image has been spoiled. Adam and Eve are now evicted from the garden, separated from God. Since this fall from grace, a relationship to God will require forgiveness and cleansing. The image of God is not removed, but it is now defaced.

The most important aspect of this defacement is that sin brought death upon them. Adam and Eve died when they ate the fruit, in the sense that their relationship to God had died. They had broken something special. And their physical death would now follow in due course. Separated from God, the source of all life, what could they do but wither and die like a plant removed from its soil? In Genesis, this is described in terms of their separation from the tree of life. Had they been able to eat from it, they might have lived for eternity, even as rebels. God expels them from the garden, so that they cannot eat this fruit of immortality. If there is one thing worse than a mortal who wants to invent morality, it is an immortal who wants to invent morality! God stopped that from happening.

This protohistory does not provide all the details we might want. For example, it is difficult to date these events. We do not know how human beings spread around the earth and when they discovered, or rediscovered, various technologies. What we do know is, whether human beings arose from Africa or from Mesopotamia, there was once an original pair, Adam and Eve, created to live in a perfect relationship without suffering or death. That relationship was broken, and now all members of the human race share a common origin and a common problem—the rebellious heart. In his Narnia chronicles, C. S. Lewis has Aslan describe the grandeur of what it is to be human in these terms:

'You come of the Lord Adam and the Lady Eve,' said Aslan. 'And that is both honour enough to erect the head of the poorest beggar, and shame enough to bow the shoulders of the greatest emperor on earth. Be content.'[13]

The biblical story of God's rescue assumes that we all share in the plight of our first parent, Adam, and he will be referred to again in these terms (Job 31:33; Hosea 6:7; Romans 5:12–21; 1 Corinthians 15:22).[14] The historicity of the fall is related to the historicity of redemption. Henri Blocher writes,

The obedience of the unique Man on that Good Friday has set free a great multitude because the evil which held us enslaved had its origin in history, and we all contracted it through the offence of the first man, on that first evil day. For a historical sin there is a historical redemption.[15]

For better and for worse, we are all born 'in Adam'. We share his glory and we share his tragedy.

Our father Abraham

The early chapters of Genesis describe the great events of our primal history—a flood that covered the earth and an attempt by a league of nations to reach up to the heavens with their Tower of Babel. These stories share the feature of illustrating humankind's attempt to live their own way, not God's. Many other great events of our primal history are not recorded in Genesis and leave only fragmentary traces in the archaeological remains, but no doubt they would only reinforce the same point. Frankly, left to our own devices, we are like spoiled children. We are capable of so much, but invariably ruin what could be good. We turn precious gold into base metal through our sin.

God's answer to this was already promised in the garden. An offspring of Eve would destroy the work of the serpent (Genesis 3:15). The family trees of Genesis lead us to one man who will become key in God's plan of salvation: Abram, a child of Terah, called to leave his home in Ur and go and live in Canaan. The Genesis text tells us only that Abram hears God's voice while the family are living in a place midway between Ur and Canaan, called Haran (Genesis 11:31). But this is not the whole story. In the New Testament, Stephen tells us that Abram heard God's call while he was still in Ur (Acts 7:2), and this would then explain why the family had already moved from Ur to Haran (Genesis 11:31). They were on their way to Canaan but, like most of us who follow God, they got waylaid.

Ur was a major town in the land of Sumer. We know from the archaeological record that it was a very early and advanced civilization, dating back beyond 3000 BC. The Bible sometimes uses a later word to refer to this region, the land of the 'Chaldeans'.[16] Because Ur was not an uncommon city name, identifying it as Ur of the Chaldeans ensured that later readers would know its location. For us, it clarifies that this is the ancient city identified from excavations in southern Iraq. It also reminds us that the book is describing much earlier events from the point of view of later Israelites.

Ur, and the civilization of Sumer, was a great centre of learning and culture in the ancient world. The archaeological finds demonstrate wealth, education, language, scientific development, music, games and beautiful artistic ability. In contrast, Canaan was undeveloped, dangerous and primitive. Abram was being called to leave a land of urban sophistication to live as a nomad in a rural backwater. As Tremper Longman describes it:

> By Abraham's time, Ur was already an ancient city, founded by Sumerians many centuries before. It was the apex of civilization. To hear the name Ur in the Ancient Near East would have the same effect as hearing New York City, London, Tokyo or some other major center of civilization. . . . Ur is a city difficult to leave.[17]

Abram's name changes to Abraham to indicate God's real purpose in his life. His former name 'exalted father' now becomes 'father of many' (Genesis 17:5). Various people groups of Canaan will be able to trace their ancestry to this wandering nomad.

Through Abraham, we have a much closer focus on a particular family in a particular place. This will remain the preoccupation of much Old Testament history. Abraham's children and their home in the land of Canaan remain the centre of attention. However, we should never lose sight of God's more global concerns. Genesis establishes that creation is a work of God, that all people are made in God's image, and that the entire human race have a heart condition known as sin, for which they deserve judgment, but from which God plans rescue. Even in the calling of a particular man, Abraham, God reaffirms his commitment that 'all peoples on earth will be blessed' (Genesis 12:3).

Finding our place

Genesis becomes our story. In particular, we can find our identity and origins in Adam and Abraham. Our identity is in Adam, because he is the father of the human race. His is the tragic story of one made in the image of God who also hides himself away from God. And that is the story of every one of us. Francis Schaeffer describes his own genealogy in this way:

> I stand in the flow of history. I know *my* origin. My lineage is longer than the Queen of England's. It does not start at the Battle of Hastings. It does not start with the beginnings of good families, wherever or whenever they lived. As I look at myself in the flow of space-time reality, I see my origin in Adam and in God's creating man in His own image.[18]

It all starts here. We are children of Adam, bearing his mark, both good and bad. But, as Christians, we are also adopted as children in Abraham's great family. In a spiritual sense, he becomes a father for all those who have faith in God (Romans 4:16). Therefore, as God promised, Abraham has become a father of a great multitude. Men and women who have come to faith in God through Christ down through history and across the continents are all children of Abraham (Galatians 3:29).

So how do we become children of Abraham? By choosing to exercise faith. By faith, we trust in what God has done in Christ to bring salvation through his death and resurrection. Abraham did not know the name Jesus as we do, but he did have the picture of the sacrifice and had to exercise trust in God. In that sense, Abraham 'saw' the day of Jesus (John 8:56). Our lives can be like Abraham's in many ways. We too may have to leave the Ur of worldly respect and achievement to face the Canaan of obscurity and uncertainty. On every step, we have to trust what God has said and that his promises are more certain than the geographical horizons before us. By faith, Abraham 'made his home in the promised land like a stranger in a foreign country; he lived in tents. . . . He was looking forward to the city with foundations, whose architect and builder is God' (Hebrews 11:9–10). We should avoid being waylaid in Haran, but set our sights on the Promised Land. Abraham is our father who has gone before us.

Bible field trip

Reading: Genesis 12:1–9
Date: 2000 BC
Destination: Canaan

1. What do you notice about Abram's journey?

2. Compare God's call (12:2) and Abram's companions (12:5). Does this suggest his obedience was compromised?

3. What does Abram do when he is in Canaan?

4. Compare God's promise to Abram (12:2–3) with God's original promise in creation (1:26–28).

5

MEET THE NATIVES

Don't travel unless you want to meet new people! Touching down in the ancient world of Canaan will bring you into contact with as cosmopolitan a collection as you might expect to see at Heathrow Airport. Remember, Canaan is the land bridge of the region. People from Africa, Asia and Europe visit, settle or just pass through. The ancient Israelites were surrounded by many other tribes and nations, all with their own cultures and religions. We are going to meet some of them now. Don't worry that they have names that seem obscure and difficult to pronounce. With a little bit of preparation, we will soon start to feel remarkably at home!

From the ground up

Adam and Eve worked the ground, and their children continued to farm and keep sheep. Agriculture was an important skill. Without it, people could only forage for food. Obviously. Because, unless you can grow and preserve crops, winters and famines will spell doom. And the development of agricultural skills went hand in hand with the development of civilization.

One essential ingredient for agriculture is a good supply of water. Wherever there is a large body of fresh water, and also regular flooding to improve the soil for crops, it is possible to start producing a surplus. And it is this surplus that allows a civilization to develop. No longer is all of life hand to mouth, but it is possible to trade from that surplus and make time to do something other than work. So there is now time to develop art, religion, philosophy and ornate public buildings. It is this very process that explains the location of two of the earliest civilizations. One arises around the River Nile and its flood valley, the other on the plain between the Tigris and Euphrates. The former becomes the location of Ancient Egypt, and the latter that of the Sumerians.

These civilizations could develop because their supply of water and flooding could be harnessed to overproduce crops and create wealth. What would you do with wealth? Well, the ancient people were just like us. Once they had it, they could turn their attention to other things—inventing gadgets and producing beautiful art, for example.

Civilization also needed space for people to live together. So the city was duly born. A Stone Age city has been found in Turkey, and we have already noted the oldest continuously inhabited city from the ancient world: Jericho in Canaan. The city becomes an important place for exchanging goods and ideas. Thankfully, the remains of many cities have survived from the ancient world, providing us with copious information about how people once lived.

The Sumerians

Much early archaeology was treasure hunting. When Sir Charles Leonard Woolley (1880–1960) began excavations at the lost city of Ur in 1922, he did something unheard of. An area was discovered that contained remains of gold and precious stones, but instead of digging there, he had that area sealed up and dug elsewhere on the site. It would be five years before he would reopen the tantalizing trench of gold. Why? Because Woolley was no treasure hunter. He wanted to understand the city they were excavating carefully and not just dig holes where he thought the treasure might be found! His patience would in time become a standard of careful archaeological practice. It also meant that he was able to identify and interpret one of the oldest urban centres in the world.

The city of Ur is nearly 7,000 years old and home to the remains of an enormous ziggurat or step pyramid. When the area that included traces of gold was finally excavated, it revealed royal tombs deep beneath the ground. These still housed beautiful royal treasures portraying the domestic and social life of Ur from 2600 BC. These treasures were buried in order to provide the dead with all they needed to continue life beyond the grave in the manner to which they were accustomed! Here was a city of sophistication and technological progress. The first examples of written language are found in Uruk and appear in Ur a few centuries later. The remains of documents written on clay include some of the earliest stories ever found, including accounts of the king who appears in the Epic of Gilgamesh.

The ancient Sumerians were indeed an intelligent people. They understood how to channel water from the rivers to irrigate their fields. They brought life to the desert. Walking in the city of Ur, you would have heard lyres, pipes and drums. And I have not even mentioned the small matter of their being credited with inventing the wheel!

And it is to this culture that we owe modern time-keeping. They used a base sixty counting system. Did they ever imagine that, thousands of years later, we would still be using the Sumerian system with our sixty-seconds-in-a-sixty-minute hour? And the 360 degrees in a circle? Yes, that was their idea too. Writing also developed among the Sumerians. But instead of pen and ink, they used a sharp-edged reed to press lines onto clay tablets that would preserve their business transactions, stories and discoveries. We call this script 'cuneiform'.

In their heyday, the Sumerians dominated the region militarily. They developed an early form of armoured chariot and trained professional solders. Trade routes from Ur would reach as far as Afghanistan and the Mediterranean.

Abraham was from Ur, and we have already met him living among the Sumerians. When Abram, as his name then was, heard God call him to leave Ur and migrate to the land of Canaan, he was being called to leave behind a technologically advanced realm to go and live as a pioneer in the west.

The Sumerian skyscraper

Hints of what we know of Sumer are found in the story of the Tower of Babel (Genesis 11:1–9). Genesis describes this as being built on a 'plain in Shinar', another name for Sumer. The people have 'one language', which may refer to the early development of language in this region. Using their cuneiform script, the Sumerians developed the skills of writing letters, textbooks and stories. But the ancient world was soon to see the rise of other languages and scripts too.

 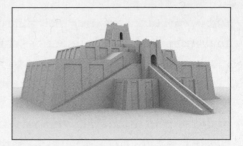

Left: photograph of the Ziggurat of Ur, taken in 1960, prior to modern reconstruction work. Right: reconstruction of the Ziggurat of Ur.

Unlike the stone pyramids of Egypt, the ziggurat was built of mud bricks, just as we read about in the Bible: '"Let's make bricks and bake them thoroughly." They used brick instead of stone, and bitumen for mortar' (Genesis 11:3). The 'tar' or 'bitumen' referred to here is a dangerously sticky substance that still oozes from the oilfields of Iraq. The ancients found it very useful for waterproofing their mud bricks. Remains of many ziggurats have been found in the region, showing that the Sumerians could teach the modern building industry a thing or two today. Fashioned from clay, their work remains visible after 4,000 years.

The attempt to build a tower into the heavens is not as far-fetched as it might seem. A sun-dried mud brick is actually very strong. Scientists have tested how high bricks can be stacked before their weight crushes those at the bottom, destroying a building's foundations. Standard mud bricks from Ur could be piled about 500 ft high, but, with a large enough base, the height could be tripled. That would have been a skyscraper in the ancient world.

However, the reference above in Genesis 11 gives us a clue as to the plans of the Sumerian architects. Instead of using sun-dried bricks, they planned to 'bake them thoroughly'. Baked bricks would have been far stronger than the sun-dried variety. In fact, scientists have found reproduction fired bricks to be *seven* times stronger than their sun-dried counterparts. In principle, a ziggurat built this way could have risen miles into the sky. The only limitation to such a plan would have been the lack of fuel to fire the number of bricks required.

In any case, the author notes that, when God wants to look at their tower reaching 'to the heavens', he must come down to see it (Genesis 11:5)! Here is a sarcastic reminder that our attempts at impressive grandeur will always look rather weedy to the God who made the galaxies.

As a result of God's judgment, the land of one language is broken, and so the scattering of nations will follow on from the division of languages. The Sumerians have their own record of this development, in a story called *Enmerkar and the Lord of Aratta*. It describes a time when all people were in unity because they spoke the same tongue, until God 'changed the speech in their mouths, [brought] contention into it, into the speech of man that *until then* had been one'."[1] It is a fleeting reference, but it echoes what we read in Genesis.

Gods of Sumer

We also know that astrology was popular in Ur. The moon represented their patron god. A temple was built at the top of the ziggurat, in order to serve the astrological gods in some way. The name of Abraham's father, Terah, was not a Hebrew name, but may be related to a Sumerian one describing a priest or prophet. But a traditional Jewish story describes Terah as an idol maker who produced his own celestial idols for the popular market.[2]

This was the region of Abraham's home town. By his time (c.2000 BC), Sumer was already in decline, and other civilizations were becoming more important, but he came from a land with a great history, as he headed into the unknown. He had been brought up in a cultured and sophisticated land, knowing about mathematics, astronomy and literature. No doubt, as a nomad in Canaan, he would in time come to miss some of the comforts and benefits of his home town.

Walk like an Egyptian

Hieroglyphics have always fascinated and inspired later cultures. Unlocking their meaning would be a key to understanding what people were thinking as they built the pyramids and paid homage to gods shaped like crocodiles and jackals. For a long time, antiquarians and scholars thought hieroglyphics might be secret spells in a pictorial form, rather than an actual language that they could translate.

But all that changed with the discovery of a broken memorial stone (stele). French forces, under Napoleon, found this in AD 1799 while at a small Egyptian town called Rosetta. They planned to return it to France for study. However, under

The Rosetta Stone, now the most popular exhibit at the British Museum in London.

the terms of the French surrender at the end of the war, it was handed over to the British, and its new home became the British Museum in London.

From its first appearance, there was no question as to its value. The broken top section of the stele was a hieroglyphic inscription. Two further blocks of text followed this section. There was an unknown cursive script, and then a block of Greek writing. The Greek was easy to read, not unlike that of the New Testament, and its translation revealed the stele to be a decree of Ptolemy V from 196 BC. Later study confirmed the hope that the same decree had been written in three parallel languages. With the Rosetta Stone as a key, the meaning of the hieroglyphs began to be unlocked. Ancient Egypt was coming to life again.

Egyptian writings include extensive king lists, which allow scholars to date the dynasties of Egypt from 3100 BC until their fall to Alexander the Great in 323 BC. After Alexander the Great came a period of Greek rulers. It was during their time that the Rosetta Stone was carved. Cleopatra was the last of these Greek rulers, and she died in 30 BC. After her, the history of Ancient Egypt would eventually be lost to memory.

Pharaohs and pyramids

Pyramid building belongs to the early period of Egyptian history. The great pyramids of Giza were built from 2700 to 2500 BC, already ancient history by the time Joseph arrived in Egypt.

While the ziggurats of Sumer served as temples, the pyramids of Egypt enclosed tombs. Unlike the mud-brick ziggurats of Sumer, the pyramids were built of stone. The pyramid of Cheops, for example, is built of 2,300,000 blocks of stone, weighing on average 2.5 tons each. That is one huge building! Not only that, but its stones fit together without cement, and it is perfectly level and aligned north. This is yet another great testament to the genius of people in the ancient world. Until a few hundred years ago, the pyramid had a smooth finish of casing stones, but these have gradually been removed. Yet it is remarkable how well such a massive building project has survived. We have certainly accrued more technology in modern times, but have we actually gained intelligence?

Israel's history is intimately entwined with that of Egypt. Abraham finds refuge here during a famine, and, through Joseph, the entire family of Israel will come to make it their home. Compared to Canaan, a visit to Egypt must have seemed like a vacation. Egypt was a land of plenty, producing a wide range of fruit, vegetables, meat and beer. Linen clothing was light and soft, ideal for a hot climate. Indeed, don't we still value Egyptian cotton to this day? Papyrus (from which our English word 'paper' is derived) was developed early on as a lightweight writing surface. Made from strips of the plant, which grows along the Nile, papyrus has survived well in the dry desert climate. This is why so many documents from this ancient empire can still be found and read until this day.

Hieroglyphic text on a scarab seal found by the author on an archeological dig near Galilee, demonstrating Egyptian influence this far north c. 1000 BC.

Egypt was ruled by a pharaoh, a title meaning 'Great House'. The Scriptures often refer to pharaoh as 'king'. A few pharaohs are mentioned by name in the Bible, including 'Shishak' (945–924 BC) who invaded Jerusalem (1 Kings 14:25–26) and 'So' (727–720 BC), who is probably Osorkon IV (2 Kings 17:1–4).

During the reign of King Hezekiah, Tirhakah (690–664 BC) went to war with Assyria (2 Kings 19:9), and Necho (610–595 BC) deposed and replaced the king of Judah, before himself being defeated by the king of Babylon (2 Kings 23:29–34). Jeremiah gives a prophecy regarding Hophra (589–570 BC), who would also face the wrath of the Babylonians (Jeremiah 44:30). These references to pharaohs all hint that, in the grand picture, Israel was only a small player caught between the confrontations of superpowers.

Egypt in the Bible

But what about the names of some more significant pharaohs? Why do we not have more from before the time of King Solomon? At the time of writing, everyone would have known who was being referred to as pharaoh, but in later years that identity has been forgotten. So we simply do not know who was pharaoh at the time of Abraham, Joseph or Moses. Yes, we would indeed like to know. But we can only make educated guesses, based on trying to harmonize the dates of Egyptian history with the Bible.

There is an interesting overlap between an important period in Ancient Egypt's history and events in the Bible. The Hyksos, an immigrant people who arrived in Egypt from about 1800 BC, eventually took control of the land until their expulsion after a revolution in 1560 BC. Who exactly were they? No one can be absolutely sure. But their name is a

Greek rendering of an Egyptian word meaning 'rulers from foreign lands'. They introduced Semitic vocabulary, bronze metalworking and better military technology, including the compound bow and the war chariot.

The period of the Hyksos overlaps with the time at which Joseph and the first of Jacob's extended family settled in Egypt, a period when it would have been possible for such foreigners to be accepted into Egyptian government and culture. While some observers go even further and identify the Hyksos with the Hebrews, it is enough to say that the Hebrews were among the Hyksos.

Of all the pharaohs' names we might wish to know, number one would be the pharaoh at the time of the exodus. Sadly, the Bible does not supply that information. But there are some clues, one of which is the dating provided by Scripture.

It is generally agreed that 1 Kings describes the dedication of Solomon's Temple in 966 BC. This is described as having taken place 'in the four hundred and eightieth year after the Israelites came out of Egypt' (1 Kings 6:1). By simple arithmetic, we could date the year of the exodus to c.1446 BC. Such arithmetic may be misleading, but a date somewhere in this region is quite plausible. Archaeologist Steven Collins has made a credible case for the dating of the exodus during the fourteenth century BC.[3]

That would place the exodus soon after the expulsion of the Hyksos and the return of native Egyptian rule. The date would explain the reference that 'a new king, to whom Joseph meant nothing, came to power in Egypt' (Exodus 1:8). If Joseph had been prominent during the period of the Hyksos, then his memory would have been lost with their expulsion.

However, another clue points to a slightly later date for the exodus. The Israelites became forced to labour under a pharaoh who used them in his own massive building projects.

The Egyptians had not used slave labour for the pyramids, but they did use slaves for later work. The Israelites did not build tombs or pyramids, but 'Pithom and Rameses as store cities for Pharaoh' (Exodus 1:11). We know that Pharaoh Rameses II oversaw major building works in Ancient Egypt. Indeed, mud bricks bearing his name have been found across the land, and his name occurs in association with many inscriptions from that time. He was the second-longest reigning king of Egypt, managing to hold onto the throne from 1279 to 1213 BC. He had eight wives and over a hundred sons. His mummified remains were found in 1881, revealing that he suffered from dreadful arthritis and dental abscesses. Like many great rulers, he was able to live a long life, but probably paid a high price in terms of chronic ill-health, for which there was little medication at that time. It might have been a mercy to die young. Many scholars think that this was the pharaoh of the exodus.

Around Canaan

God says to Abram that he will give to his descendants 'this land, from the Wadi of Egypt to the great river, the Euphrates—the land of the Kenites, Kenizzites, Kadmonites, Hittites, Perizzites, Rephaites, Amorites, Canaanites, Girgashites and Jebusites' (Genesis 15:18–21). That is the kind of passage you do not want to be asked to read out loud in a church service! However, this is only one of seventeen similar lists in the Bible, covering the inhabitants of Canaan before the arrival of the Israelites. About some of these people groups we know a great deal; of others we know next to nothing. Genesis identifies the Canaanites as the descendants of Ham (Genesis 10:15–18). They were distantly related tribal groups scattered about the region.

Cities of Canaan

One of the marked features of the early culture of Canaan is the rise of the city during the Early Bronze Age.[4] Each city would have had a king, not unlike a mayor, who governed their city and outlying villages. Though these cities may have been independent kingdoms, there was a clear Canaanite culture of language and customs throughout the region. Language, music and fashions developed in these urban centres.

But Canaan also harboured a dark religious tradition. It was typical practice to use a mountain or build a stone structure as a 'high place' where sacrifices could be offered. Worship practice, sadly, even included human sacrifice and the use of ritual prostitutes.

The cities were fortified and rose high above the surrounding plains. Their fortifications tell us that these were dangerous times. Prior to the exodus, Jericho was about 3 hectares (7.5 acres in size), while Hazor spread to 80 hectares. (By way

Canaanite settler playing a lyre,
from the Egyptian Beni Hasan tomb.

Archaeologists have uncovered the shrine at Dan. The modern metal structure marks the location of the altar.

of comparison, a soccer field is about 1 hectare in size.) Thick walls with watchtowers provided the main line of defence. During the Bronze Age, Jericho had a population of 2,500, while Hazor had 40,000. Imagining what these cities were like can be misleading, given our experience in the contemporary world. Alan Millard provides the following caution:

> The word 'city', for example, is widely used for the Akkadian *ālum* and for Hebrew *'îr* when a small town is meant—Jericho was not a city like London, Liverpool, New York, or Chicago, but more like one of the small mediaeval walled towns of Tuscany or the Near East.[5]

The houses, palace, market and roadways would have been tightly compacted, and even a small population must have been crowded.

Within Canaan, there were other smaller tribal groups, including the Perizzites and Jebusites. They were probably all loosely related descendants of Ham. While dialects varied by region, there was a common use of the Semitic language. Of particular interest to us is the fact that they shared the word for the highest God, El, which would be preserved by the Israelites in their Scriptures.

Mysterious Melchizedek

Up in the mountains, far from the coast,[6] lay a small town on a ridge near the desert wilderness. A Canaanite tribe called the Jebusites had settled in this isolated spot. Their city, Jebus (Judges 19:10–11), had a population of about 2,000, ruled by their city king. The most fascinating of their kings is the mysterious Melchizedek (Genesis 14:18–19).[7] After Abram had fought to rescue his nephew, Lot, he returns to the hill country and is met by the king of 'Salem', who shares in worship of God (El) and receives a tenth of Abram's spoils of war. Salem is another name for Jebus, the city that would one day be called Jerusalem.

Melchizedek brings Abram 'bread and wine'. Sharing a communal meal is a way of declaring peace between potential rivals. That can still work today. If you fall out with someone and need to build bridges, you might not offer them bread and wine, but you might well take them out for a meal! Melchizedek is forming an agreement with Abram. By giving a portion of his bounty to Melchizedek, Abram is recognizing this agreement and submitting to his status.

There is also a theological agreement between them. Melchizedek, a Canaanite 'priest of God Most High', blesses Abram in the name of El, the Most High God. The knowledge of God from the time of Noah had been passed down from Ham to at least some of his descendants. Here was one Canaanite chief who retained knowledge of the God of creation. There may have been others too. However, this residual righteousness was not to last. The dreadful practices of so many Canaanites would become the more common theme.

Long-lost peoples

The list of people in Genesis 15 includes the Amorites. In the east, they formed a great empire in Babylon, though others were settled in Canaan. Likewise, the Hittites were a great empire to the north, in Anatolia (modern-day Turkey). But many Hittite families also settled in the land of Canaan, and we read that Abram bought a burial cave from the Hittites (Genesis 23).[8]

The Bible describes the Canaanites as being punished by God when the Israelites conquered the land. The exact timing of the Joshua campaign was to fit the period predicted by God. The people of Canaan would come to deserve this judgment: 'In the fourth generation your descendants will come back here, for the sin of the Amorites has not yet reached its full measure' (Genesis 15:16). By the time of Joshua, the righteousness of Melchizedek would have been only a distant memory.

The Philistines

The Philistines were settlers who arrived in the land during the Late Bronze Age and into the Iron Age. They came from the Greek islands, especially Crete.[9] As a sea people, their interests lay along the coastal plain. What we call the Mediterranean could even be called the Sea of the Philistines (Exodus 23:31). They were seafarers who could trade and wage war on the open sea.

The Philistines were a force to be reckoned with. As traders, they were up to date with the latest technology. They mastered Iron Age metalwork. They had chariots and fine pottery. Far from being uncultured, they had brought the sophistication of early Greek culture with them. In a contest, Israel were the underdogs (1 Samuel 13:19–21). The modern expression

'Philistine', used to describe someone who lacks culture or cares little for art, is unfair to these advanced sea peoples.

While the richer lands of the coastal plain were in the hands of the Philistines, the Israelites were able to retain the more easily defended hill and mountain country. By a curious dint of history, after a Jewish revolt was suppressed in AD 135, the Roman Emperor Hadrian renamed the province of Judea as Palestine, after the Philistines. This would remain its name for 2,000 years. Palestinian is the Latin form of the word 'Philistine,' and so we have an echo of these ancient peoples today.

The rise of Assyria

Along the Tigris-Euphrates River Valley, various powers developed their imperial ambitions. In the north, the Assyrian Empire came to threaten the nations of Canaan.

For much of its history, the northern kingdom of Israel was considered a tribute state to Assyria. The Black Obelisk of Assyrian King Shalmaneser III (reigned 858–824 BC) includes a depiction of King Jehu, 'son' of Omri, and fellow Israelites bringing tribute to the king.

The Black Obelisk of Shalmaneser III provides the earliest image of ancient Israelites. King Jehu, or his representative, is bowing down before the Assyrian king (841 BC).

The Bible mentions a number of Assyrian kings by name, including Tiglath-Pileser III (2 Kings 15:29) and a later Shalmaneser (2 Kings 17:3).

Tiglath-Pileser III was also known as 'Pul' (2 Kings 15:19), and the author of Kings is aware that these two names describe the same person. An attempt by Israel to rebel against Assyria by joining with Egypt only leads to a crushing invasion and complete defeat (2 Kings 17:5).

Assyria brought the northern kingdom to an end in 722 BC. The Assyrians deported other people from the east and settled them in this region. With their capital in Samaria, they had become known as the Samaritans by the time of the New Testament.

The southern kingdom of Judah does not escape the attention of the Assyrians either. King Ahaz (reigned c.735–715 BC) had made Judah subject to Assyria, so when his son Hezekiah rebelled against them, he aroused the wrath of the Assyrians. King Sennacherib (reigned c.704–681 BC) laid siege to Jerusalem during the time of King Hezekiah (2 Kings 18–20), and the brutality of his campaign in the nearby city of Lachish is grimly pictured on an expansive wall relief now housed at the British Museum. Their treatment of defeated enemies was always brutal and cruel. Rebels were inevitably treated harshly. However, in the case of Hezekiah, Jerusalem withstands this particular siege.

Jonah's journey

The centre of the Assyrian Empire contained four major cities: Ashur, Nineveh, Calah and Khorsabad. These were large and prosperous. Remember that Jericho was about 3 hectares in size? Enormous Hazor, in northern Canaan, grew to 80 hectares. Visiting Assyrian cities would have been an overwhelming experience! Nineveh, for example, expanded to 730 hectares in size. Jonah made a 550-mile journey from the Mediterranean to Nineveh. He arrived in a city that required a three-day visit (Jonah 3:3). That is not the time it would have taken to walk around the perimeter, but the time to visit the gates and temples.

However, the empire of Assyria at the time of Jonah was not to last. There was a new kid on the block. Nineveh fell to the Babylonian Empire in 612 BC. The Assyrian army was all but destroyed by the Babylonians, who took control of the region.

By the waters of Babylon

Babylon was an ancient city that rose and fell in significance more than once. Its name means 'Gate of God', and it was the location of an impressive brick ziggurat, which would have dominated the horizon. A Hebrew wordplay on the name reminds us that this was the location for the confusion of languages (Genesis 11:9). The English-speaking world continues to use the word 'babble' to describe a confusion of voices. When we use this word, we are retaining a reminder of this once-great city.

The literature of the Babylonians covers a breadth of subjects with a depth of thought. Poetry, mathematics, medicine, astronomy and historical chronicles are all preserved on the clay tablets found in excavations. Travellers to its capital city would have been awed by impressive architecture adorned with beautiful glazed tiles. And what of the Hanging Gardens of Babylon, a wonder of the ancient world?

The Seven Wonders of the World was a 'must-see-before-you-die' list, drawn up in classical Greece. Of that list only the Pyramid of Giza remains. But the legend of the Hanging

Gardens relies on descriptions of a large raised platform, supported by pillars, on which flowers and trees grew. The Babylonians would certainly have had the technology and inclination to build such gardens. Their irrigation technology was able to divert waters where they wished and bring life to the desert.

Come and join us

The Babylonian treatment of enemies certainly included violence, but they also recognized the importance of what is called 'assimilation'. If you assimilate your enemies into your own customs and culture, they will no longer have anything to rebel against. Once you started eating Babylonian food, listening to their latest music and wearing their fashions, you really would start to wonder what you were rebelling against. So the attempt was made to assimilate the people of Judah into Babylon.

This policy is evident in the book of Daniel. The Babylonians chose him and his friends, 'Israelites from the royal family and the nobility' (Daniel 1:3), in order to train them in 'the language and literature of the Babylonians' (Daniel 1:4) for a period of three years. They were even given Babylonian names. They were treated well and given royal food and wine, along with a promise of no tuition fees! But it all reflected a deliberate Babylonian policy to erase national identity and cement Babylonian supremacy. And it failed. The Jewish identity, even without a temple, only became clearer during this stage. Long after Babylon had become ancient history, the Jews continued to follow their own language and literature. I know of plenty of children still given the popular name Daniel, but I have yet to meet one with the name Belteshazzar!

Out of Persia

Old Testament history draws to a close with the rise of Persia. Its capital, even farther east than Babylon, in modern-day Iran, had difficulties maintaining interests so far west as Judah. The king of Persia, Cyrus, allowed the Jews, along with other people groups, to return to their homelands in the wake of the fall of Babylon.

This Persian policy is recorded on an important clay cylinder. The decree of Cyrus in 539 BC, to allow deported peoples to return to their lands and rebuild their homes and temples, was inscribed in cuneiform. This decree provides the context for the one we read about in Ezra 1:1–4. It fits the same benign political atmosphere. Cyrus saw himself as being raised up by the gods to allow the local shrines and temples of the region to be rebuilt. The policy of King Cyrus is considered so enlightened that a copy of the cylinder is housed at the headquarters of the United Nations and hailed as the first charter of human rights. This is generally thought to be a bit of an overstatement, but the decree certainly endorses religious freedoms.

The book of Esther sees a Jewish woman who married into the royal family of Persia at home in Persia and able to influence government in favour of protecting the Jews from an attempted genocide. Back in Judah, we read of Nehemiah and Ezra helping to promote the rebuilding work on the walls, homes and temple of Jerusalem. The nation would never regain the prestige or independence of their time under the united monarchy of Solomon, but they would retain their identity through the rise and fall of surrounding nations.

Those silent years

The period after these books close until the writing of the Gospels are sometimes called the silent years. They are silent as far as the writing of Scripture is concerned, and 400 years will elapse between the last Old Testament book and the writing of the first books of the New Testament. However, those years were far from being silent. Judah was caught up in a power struggle between Persia and Greece. In their wake came the mighty Roman Empire, which would dominate the region during the New Testament period.

Exploring ancient times means encountering various peoples. Tribal bonds and ancestral loyalty meant that these groups could be tight-knit. But they did communicate, integrate and learn from one another. When we explore the ancient world with the Bible, we should be aware of these differences. But we should not be put off. They were all people much like us. They sang, played, loved and lost. Life could be hard, and people treated brutally, but the same human heart pulsed through it all. And the same God is at work today as was at work among them so long ago.

Bible field trip

Reading: 1 Samuel 17:1–58
Date: 1020 BC
Destination: Valley, south-west of Jerusalem

1. How have the armies prepared for battle, and what is Goliath demanding?

2. How does the description of Goliath's armour help us understand the Philistines?

3. What equipment and experience does David bring to the battle?

4. To what does David attribute his victory?

6

AMONG MANY GODS

To be successful time travellers, we need to learn to think as the ancient peoples did. Why did they build altars, mummify the dead, circumcise young boys and sacrifice animals? It may all look rather odd to us. But it reflects what these people believed about the supernatural realm. How many gods are mentioned in the Bible? One? Actually, you can count over thirty deities mentioned by name. Let's equip ourselves with a brief overview.

The one God

El is the most common Hebrew name for God. It's a word not unique to the Israelites, and is used in a similar way to the English noun 'god' in the range of deities to which it may be applied. But if the word can be used quite generally throughout the region, how do we know to which god someone is referring?

Over 200 times, the Hebrew writers extend the description to draw attention to the uniqueness of their God. For example, one common variant is *El Elyon*, meaning God Most High. Interestingly, there is also a plural version of the name in the Bible: *Elohim*. However, this does not mean that Genesis is describing 'gods' rather than God. *Elohim* is plural, but used with verbs that are singular. It is as if the Hebrew writer wanted to use the highest, most all-encompassing title for the one God, and so chose this plural noun. Not surprisingly, Christians see this as a glimpse of the Trinity in the very first chapter of the Bible, the one God who is three persons.

Know my name

The personal name of this God is Yahweh. God reveals his name and its meaning to Moses (Exodus 3:13–15). By the time of Jesus, the Israelites were not pronouncing the name aloud, and so we do not really know how it originally sounded. When they came across the word in their readings of Scripture, they would substitute an alternative word meaning 'Lord'. But did the patriarchs know God by this name? Exodus suggests not: 'I appeared to Abraham, to Isaac and to Jacob as God Almighty, but by my name the LORD I did not make myself known to them' (Exodus 6:3). However, we do find the name being used in Genesis (4:26; 14:22). A common explanation of this, from both Jews and Christians, is that a Hebrew name is much more than a label. To use the label or word 'Yahweh', as the patriarchs did, is not the same as to understand the meaning of that name. Abraham called God 'Yahweh', but to Moses the significance of that name was given: 'I am who I am.'[1]

Monotheism is the belief that there is only one God. Some theologians have tried to deny that the early Israelites were monotheists and suggest rather that Genesis assumes polytheism (belief in many gods). After all, many different names are used for God. However, the various names all refer to the same God. Abram swears an oath to 'the LORD [*Yahweh*], God Most High [*El Elyon*], Creator of heaven and earth' (Genesis 14:22). However, we do not have to read far in the Old Testament before we encounter other gods, many of whom have personal names. Who are these gods and, perhaps most importantly, are they real?

Other gods?

While Jacob is staying with his father-in-law, there is a curious incident in which his wife Rachel decides to steal 'her father's household gods' (Genesis 31:19). These gods (Hebrew *teraphim*) were little idols kept in the Canaanite homes and used as objects of worship or lucky charms. Houses probably had domestic shrines and maybe more than one god, just to be on the safe side. Why does Rachel decide to steal them? They could be used as proof of family identity, like a passport in the ancient world, and property ownership. Rachel was probably going to use them not for worship, but as evidence of her rights to property. It is another question altogether whether Jacob and Rachel believed these gods to be real beings. The world of the Old Testament is polytheistic, but the Israelites were called to worship one God only.

The Israelites must continue dealing with rival gods, even as they settle the land. Jephthah, one of Israel's judges, is brought into a conflict with the neighbouring kingdom of Ammon. He compares their god, Chemosh, with Yahweh: 'Will you not take what your god Chemosh gives you? Likewise, whatever the LORD our God has given us, we will possess' (Judges 11:24). Jephthah is telling the Ammonites to back off. Yahweh has given his people this land, just as Chemosh had given the Ammonites their own land. Jephthah seems to be a muddled theologian at this point. For one thing, Chemosh was the national god of Moab, not of Ammon. But even more importantly, does Jephthah really believe in the existence of Chemosh? Some religious scholars describe the early sections of the Old Testament as 'monolatrous' rather than monotheistic. What they mean is that the Israelites privileged their one god above all others, without necessarily denying the existence of other gods. Was this true of Jephthah's reference to Chemosh? Did he worship one God while believing in the existence of many others?

The simplest explanation is probably the best: Jephthah really is muddled in his theology! He identifies the wrong god for the Ammonites and supports polytheism: 'Jephthah's obvious contempt for his antagonists undoubtedly contributed to the hostile response his speech received. But in this comment Jephthah also displayed contempt for his own theological traditions.'[2] Jephthah believed in Yahweh, but he probably also affirmed the existence of other national gods, and that was part of his problem. When it comes to theology, the judges of the book that bears their name do not inspire great confidence!

Downgrading religion

Genesis describes a decline from monotheism into polytheism. Adam and Eve, along with their immediate family, worship the one true God. But then things go horribly adrift! As theologian of religions, Dan Strange, remarks, 'From Genesis 3 onwards we are able to trace both theologically and historically the human reaction to this divine revelation, in other words, the history of human religion, both its preservation and degeneration, both its progress and regress.'[3] Genesis provides a record of the origins of the world religions.

Other gods, many gods, weather gods, national gods and ancestral gods quickly appear on the scene. They tell us little about supernatural reality, but a great deal about human psychology. Our natural instinct is to create gods in the image of things we see around us. In the New Testament, Paul observed this instinct in classical Roman and Greek culture (Romans 1:25).

Jeremiah, the Old Testament prophet, delivered this verdict:

> Do people make their own gods?
>   Yes, but they are not gods!
> (Jeremiah 16:20)

Even the psalmist can sing that the Lord is 'to be feared above all gods' and then he adds,

> For all the gods of the nations are idols,
>   but the LORD made the heavens.
> (Psalm 96:4–5)

So let us meet the gods of the ancient world with this in mind. Not everything is at it seems.

Gods of Egypt

In the early period of Bible history, Egypt was the dominant power in the region. Her religion was very influential. Apart from a brief period of monotheism, Egypt paid homage to over 700 different deities. These gods reflected aspects of the natural environment. The movement of the sun, the waters of the Nile and the death of the body all had supernatural significance. From inscriptions and statues, we glimpse the images of these gods, such as Sobek, the crocodile-headed god of creation, and Ra, the sun god, whose disc sits atop a man with the head of a falcon.

The blending of humans, animals and symbols does make sense. Sobek is associated with creation, as it was thought a crocodile was first to emerge from the life-giving Nile. For an Egyptian, life depended on the River Nile, and in the cool of an early morning sunrise, an Egyptian might watch as the massive bulk of a crocodile emerged from the waters. This gave a sense of life emerging in the primordial creation. The sun, Ra, dominated all of life as it glided across the sky, unobstructed by the more frequent clouds of northern Europe. No doubt an Egyptian looking skyward would often catch a glimpse of a falcon soaring across the sky. Horus was the natural association of the falcon with the sun.

For us, the images of jackals, crocodiles and falcons can be sinister and disturbing, but they made sense to the Egyptians. Egyptian religion had a strong sense of the balance between order and chaos. By serving and pleasing the gods through offerings and justice, order could be maintained, and the crops would come in season. By failing to serve the gods, chaos could reign and starvation might well come.

An important god in Egyptian mythology was Pharaoh himself. The Egyptians considered their pharaoh to be a descendant of the gods. Therefore, along with the gods of the world around them, Pharaoh would have to be served and brought pleasure. A convenient arrangement for the pharaoh!

The heretical pharaoh

The proliferation of Egyptian gods was brought to an abrupt, though temporary, end under Pharaoh Akhenaten (reigned c.1353–1335 BC). This mysterious king turned Egypt away from its panoply of gods to a form of monotheism. Born

Amenhotep IV, he had been brought up in the traditional Egyptian religious ways. However, on coming to the throne, he abolished the worship of the ancient gods and imposed a single god upon the people. He also broke up the priesthood and moved the capital away from historic Karnak to a new city, Amarna. He changed his name to reflect the new religion. Akhenaten, meaning 'the living spirit of the Aten', identified the sun (Aten was another name for Ra) as the one god to be worshipped. A new style of art briefly flowered in Egypt, more lifelike and domestic. The rays of the sun disc replaced the powers of the many gods. Two thousand years of Egyptian polytheism had ended.

With the death of Akhenaten, his religious reformation quickly unravelled. Under Tutankhamun, traditional religion was restored, and his memory was almost erased from Egyptian records.

Scholars find it hard to explain this brief period of monotheism. Is there a connection between Akhenaten and the Israelites? Possibly, but it is not clear exactly what that connection may be! Given an early date for the exodus, it is possible that Akhenaten's brief reforms follow the devastating plagues.

Mysterious Pharaoh Akhenaten of the 18th Dynasty, with his family.

Some scholars even speculate that Akhenaten may have been the son of the pharaoh of the exodus. He was not the first-born or natural heir—Akhenaten's older brother had died young. However, if the exodus happened a little later, as many scholars believe, then these religious reforms would have taken place just before the birth of Moses. If so, perhaps the influence of the Israelites living in the land had already been felt by Pharaoh. That would add to the hostility of a later polytheistic pharaoh towards the monotheistic Israelites. Their desire to go out into the desert to worship their god might have sounded strangely like Akhenaten's relocation from Karnak to his desert capital during his religious revolution.

Gods of Canaan

Walk into any major city of ancient Canaan and you pass by large stones guarding the gates, bearing the images of various local gods. Each city has a divine representative, and you are expected to pay your respects at the gate. Baal (also known as Hadad) was the god of the storm. Baal is a title meaning 'Lord' or 'Master', and he was the most popular god across the region, being worshipped throughout Canaan. As the god of the storm, he brought destruction and demonstrated his power, but he also brought rain and was associated with fertility. The Old Testament uses the plural form, 'Baals' (1 Kings 18:18), which suggests there were many local pagan versions of Baal across the region.

Dagon was the father of Baal and, traditionally, thought to be a fish-like god. This reflects the Hebrew meaning of the name, and various pagan images have been found of a fish-tailed god. No one can be sure of this link, though it is possible. Dagon was the primary god of the Philistines. In the heart of the land of Canaan they built a large temple to Dagon in a city called Beth Shan. When King Saul was defeated by the Philistines at nearby

Mount Gilboa, they brought his body to this city and placed his head in 'the temple of Dagon' (1 Chronicles 10:10).

Because of the gods' associations with grain, fish and harvest, some people think that they were peaceful gods. However, that would be a great misunderstanding. Baal and Dagon were actually bloodthirsty gods of war. But they were mild compared to a third god, worshipped by the Ammonites.

The dark side

Molech (NIV 'Molek') was worshipped by the Ammonites (1 Kings 11:7) and throughout Canaan, and even the ancient Israelites were drawn to worship him. This worship included the grisly practice of child sacrifice. The Old Testament alludes to the use of a 'fire' for the worship of Molech (2 Kings 23:10). The worship of Baal and Molech probably shared this cruel practice (Jeremiah 32:35).[4] And we have hints of this in the archaeological record.

The Phoenician sea people settled on the Mediterranean coast, including Tyre in Canaan and Carthage in Tunisia, North Africa, and a number of ancient writers, including Plutarch and Philo, refer to the disturbing practice of child sacrifice in Carthage. During one particular siege, historians record that as many as 200

The remains of the baby cemetery at Carthage.

children of noble families were offered as sacrifices. Archaeologists have discovered an enormous child cemetery with the remains of sacrificial victims. Dating from about 400 BC, 20,000 urns have been recovered, containing the charred remains of children under the age of two. This truly horrific discovery speaks of a time when young babies may well have been offered as sacrifices in fire. Their remains were interred in a soccer-field–sized cemetery. Plutarch (c.46–120 AD), writing after the Old Testament period, records this description of the practice in Carthage:

> With full knowledge and understanding they themselves offered up their own children, and those who had no children would buy little ones from poor people and cut their throats as if they were so many lambs or young birds; meanwhile the mother stood by without a tear or moan; but should she utter a single moan or let fall a single tear, she had to forfeit the money, and her child was sacrificed nevertheless.[5]

Worshipping pagan deities demanded human sacrifice. This was one of the reasons why the peoples of ancient Canaan were destroyed at the time of Joshua. Long before the events of the exodus, God had revealed to Abraham that, by the time of his descendant Joshua, their sin would have reached its full measure (see Genesis 15:16). Yahweh wanted no compromise with the gods of Canaan. To make peace with the gods of the ancient world was to destroy worship of the true God. The Israelites had been warned to avoid any interreligious worship. They even had to be warned not to offer their children as sacrifices (Leviticus 18:3), a lesson that should already have been learned from Abraham. When the Patriarch was called by God to offer his son Isaac on Mount Moriah, he was being taught a lesson, learning to trust God. It was also an opportunity for God to demonstrate and underline the principle of substitution: a ram to be offered in place of the child Isaac. Only animals and grain would be acceptable sacrifices before Yahweh.

Sadly, the ancient Israelites were continually drawn to the worship of other gods, especially Baal. Remember, it was with the prophets of Baal that Elijah had to contend on Mount Carmel (1 Kings 18). It is hard to believe that the Israelites would even come to dabble in the worship of Molech! King Solomon built an altar to this god on the Mount of Olives, and King Ahaz offered his own children 'in the fire' (2 Chronicles 28:3). For all the Bible's teaching on purity of devotion to Yahweh, the Old Testament is very realistic about people being attracted to the pagan gods. This has led to a very real mismatch between what the Bible says the Israelites should have been doing and what we find they actually got up to. As a time traveller to the ancient world, you would have had many reasons to berate the Israelites for ignoring the commandments of God and compromising their faith with the world around them. But then, is it not also true that the same rebuke has to be made of our own churches today? There is another aspect of Israelite worship that fell far short of what the Bible called them to.

Did God have a wife?

How do you sell a book? Give it a provocative title. Archaeologist William Dever and his publishers certainly did that with *Did God Have a Wife?* in 2005. Dever presented 'evidence' that, in ancient Israel, Yahweh had a sexual consort. Of course, he did not mean that she actually existed; indeed, even Yahweh may not have existed. His point was only that, in the worship life of the Israelites, there was evidence that some people believed Yahweh had a female consort. So what is this evidence?

As an archaeologist, Dever is concerned to allow texts other than the Bible to speak with equal authority. The Bible is taken to be only one perspective, perhaps the official one, on life in ancient Israel. What do we learn from other literary texts and material artifacts from that time? What Dever calls 'folk religion' is the everyday religious life of the Israelites, and at certain important points, that folk religion parts company with the official line.

If Yahweh were to have a wife, then he would not have to look far in the mythology of ancient Canaan. Asherah was a popular goddess in Late Bronze Age culture, around the time when the Israelites were in Egypt. She would have been worshipped by many of the Israelites. In Elijah's confrontation with the prophets of Baal on Mount Carmel, there were almost as many prophets of Asherah with them (1 Kings 18:19). The good kings and judges are frequently involved in cutting down wooden Asherah poles erected by idolatrous Israelites (e.g., 2 Chronicles 34:5–7).[6]

Outside the Bible, Dever identifies two important ancient Hebrew inscriptions: one found at Kuntillet 'Ajrud, in Sinai, and the other from Judea. They are both blessings referring to Yahweh and 'his Asherah'. The example from Kuntillet 'Ajrud has the added feature of an accompanying drawing that might show a male Yahweh with a female consort and a musician seated nearby. With this evidence for a married Yahweh, Dever seeks to explain a particular object frequently found in ancient Israelite excavations.

The object is a figurine, obviously female, and often associated with fertility. Could this be an Asherah, consort of Yahweh? Dever thinks so. Putting the evidence together, he suggests that the folk religion of Israelites had a male Yahweh with a female companion, Asherah, and together they were worshipped.

Dever may well be mistaken. By the time of the Hebrew Bible, the word 'Asherah' simply denotes a wooden pole used in worship. In the forty references to Asherah in the Bible, it is unclear that any refer to the Bronze Age goddess of that name. The picture of a male and female figure from Kuntillet 'Ajrud does not belong to the accompanying inscription; it is a crude cartoon drawn much later. Generally, scholars believe they are pictures of Bes, an Egyptian deity, and unrelated to Yahweh. It is pure guesswork to connect them with the inscription. Furthermore, there is no textual evidence that the female figurines found in Israel represent Asherah.[7]

However, Dever's general suggestion that Israel had a folk religion that countenanced the idea of Yahweh having a wife need not be all that controversial. Israelites worshipped other gods and indulged in various immoral sexual practices. As we know, the Bible records this. But the prophets frequently condemned it. It was partly for this sin that God brought judgment upon them. One of the repeated words of God against the Israelite leaders was that they too dabbled in the worship of foreign gods. Against this backdrop, the idea that the people indulged in some kind of pluralism in their worship seems entirely plausible.

Demons of the ancient world

As we have seen in our encounter with Molech, many of the gods of the ancient world were disturbingly cruel and capricious. This leads to the question: were these the demons described in the New Testament?

The name Baal-Zebub appears in the Old Testament as the god of Ekron (2 Kings 1). It is an odd name, because it simply means 'Lord of the Flies'. It is possible that this is a Hebrew play on words. The original title was something like 'Prince Baal'. However, the Old Testament pun draws attention to his real nature. Far from being a god of life and harvest, this is the god of death and decay, where the flies gather. In the New Testament, this name is taken up as a name for Satan, the Prince of Demons (Matthew 10:25).

The Old Testament does provide direct references to the activity of Satan (Job 1:6; 1 Chronicles 21:1). Though he cannot kill, he tempts and lies and leads people to their destruction. He inspires arrogance and detracts from God. That Baal, Dagon and Molech were suitable masks for him to wear makes perfect sense. The Hebrew name, Satan, means 'adversary', and he is Enemy Number One to Yahweh.

Who is Satan?

Jesus draws upon Isaiah 14:12–15 to describe the fall of Satan from heaven at the beginning of creation (Luke 10:18). In context, the prophet Isaiah seems to be describing the arrogance of the king of Babylon. However, in order to condemn a historical king, Isaiah raises his vision to see a greater, cosmic parallel:

> How you have fallen from heaven,
> morning star, son of the dawn!
> You have been cast down to the earth,
> you who once laid low the nations!
> You said in your heart,
> 'I will ascend to the heavens;
> I will raise my throne
> above the stars of God;
> I will sit enthroned on the mount of assembly,
> on the utmost heights of Mount Zaphon.
> (Isaiah 14:12–13)

The 'morning star' may be a reference to Venus, an astral deity worshipped in the ancient world, and the planet that appears brightly in the early-morning sky. However, the Hebrew is more simply rendered: 'Shining One', and refers to the splendour of this being, comparable to a beautiful star. The Latin translation of this Hebrew word is 'Lucifer', from which we have one of Satan's many names. Mount Zaphon was understood, outside the Bible, to be the throne of Baal. Zaphon simply means 'northern' and probably identifies a mountain near Ugarit in Syria. This was Baal's home base, and all the local Baals were somehow connected to this source. But the Shining One does not retain his place of privilege. He is thrown down to earth and becomes the lord of the dead and the depths of the pit. Who is Isaiah referring to? Three different beings are in view: a historical king, the pagan divinity called Baal, and Satan. It is as if Satan's rise and fall become reenacted in the lives of every false god and godless king throughout history.

Another insight into Satan is found in Ezekiel 28:12–19. The prophet is speaking of the king of Tyre, but he places the king's arrogance in a cosmic context. The figure of Ezekiel's vision was perfect in wisdom and beauty, clothed in jewels (another 'Shining One'?). He was in Eden from creation, but through pride was cast down, and his destiny is destruction in fire. While we are not directly told that this figure is Satan, it has seemed a natural meaning to many. Who inspires the king of Tyre? Who inspired the king of Babylon? Down through history, the ultimate role model for pagan rulers has been Satan.

The uniqueness of the Lord

If you time travelled to the earliest periods of the Old Testament and met with Abraham or David, then you would realize that their monotheism was a radical idea. Everyone felt the pull to worship or please the various pagan deities across the region. Whether the stars above or the creatures below, people found objects of devotion all around. In contrast, monotheism developed and became more refined as the Scriptures unfolded.

The many deities of the Old Testament world reflect the fact of religious pluralism. People worshipped many different gods and still do so to this day. In that sense, pluralism is a fact like gravity! However, the biblical writers do not endorse pluralism. In their devotion to Yahweh, they recognize that the other gods are either demons or the product of human imagination. Idols tell us a great deal about the human heart, but very little about the supernatural realm.

John Day, surveying the array of deities across that region during ancient times, concludes,

> Everything became transformed in the light of monotheism, and it is arguably monotheism . . . rather than God's mighty acts in history as used to be argued, that most distinguishes the Old Testament from the religions of the other nations of the ancient Near East.[8]

Contemporary Jews repeat the great summary statement of Old Testament theology every day. It is called the 'Shema', which is the first Hebrew word of the phrase: 'Hear, O Israel: the LORD our God, the LORD is one' (Deuteronomy 6:4). Other pagan documents make the claim that their God is 'one'. This need only mean that, as a people, they are willing to worship only one god, regardless of the existence of others. The Shema makes a greater statement: God is unique; God is incomparable; no other gods are fit for worship.

The Israelites worshipped one God, but were always in danger of falling for pretenders. This was why God created what might seem like an elaborate system of ritual and law for them. It makes sense in the light of the polytheism of the ancient world. The long, legal framework given at the time of Moses provides a ring of protection around the exclusive loyalty the Israelites were called to show to Yahweh. However, this legal framework used concepts and objects already known in the ancient world. Many of the laws, rituals and punishments were common outside Israel. But those similarities are now set in a new context of devotion to the faithful God. In this new setting, similar laws and rituals take on new meaning, as they express the possibility of a living relationship of love with God and fellow humanity. Commenting on the Old Testament's uniqueness, John Oswalt observes,

> It is not unique because it is not part of its world; neither is it unique because its writers are incapable of relating what they say to that world. Rather, it is unique precisely because being a part of its world and using concepts and forms from its world, it can project a vision of reality diametrically opposite to the vision of that world.[9]

To pursue this theme a little further, we can consider the ark and the tabernacle. When Moses left Egypt, he was given detailed instructions for building a portable sanctuary, the tabernacle, and a wooden box to hold the tablets of the law, the ark. Such items were already well known in Egypt. Among the treasures of Tutankhamun, located by archaeologist Howard Carter, were found portable shrines and a sacred box with poles for its transportation.[10] The tabernacle used by the Israelites was a wooden-framed tent, 15 by 45 ft. Under the outer coverings of ram skins and goat hair curtains, there would have been two very dark rooms. The first, or Holy Place, was twice the length of a smaller inner room, or Holy of Holies, in which the ark of the covenant was placed. The whole structure could be folded up like a tent and carried with the Israelites as they travelled through the desert.

The most striking parallel to the tabernacle that has yet emerged is found on a wall relief of Rameses II from the battle of Kadesh. This relief shows a tent structure, oriented, like Egyptian monumental architecture, towards the east. The outer structure creates a large open space in which the central tent is assembled. The tent itself has two rooms, a larger reception room and a smaller throne room for Rameses II. It is striking that both the outer area and the tent itself are rectangular—just like the tabernacle of Moses. Most camps in ancient history were understandably oval, a better use of space, and for the Israelite tribes camping around the tabernacle, such a structure would have made a lot of sense. But the description given in the Bible is remarkably like the tabernacle of Rameses II in thirteenth-century Egypt.

The proportions of the Egyptian tabernacle are similar to those given by God to Moses. The wall relief shows Rameses sitting in his inner room, flanked by two winged Horus deities. The similarities with the tabernacle of Moses are obvious. God used a pattern, not unknown at that time, for the Israelites to follow in building their own temple structure. However, regardless of similarities, the differences are key. The Egyptian tent led visitors into the presence of a god-like pharaoh, flanked by the wings of the falcon god. The Israelite Holy of Holies was house for the Word of God, his law, flanked by the guardian cherubim. No human or created image could take God's place. And only through sacrifice could a priest come before the utterly unique God and represent sinful Israel.[11]

As the tabernacle deteriorated over time, David saw the need to build a permanent stone structure to replace it. The decision to site it in Jersualem was strategic, and the architecture reflected the plan already given by God for the tabernacle. It was left to David's son, King Solomon, to conduct the building work itself. But the temple design was not entirely unique to Israel. Archaeologists have never been able to conduct a detailed excavation of the Temple Mount to reveal what temple remains might still be found. On its approximate location stands the Islamic Dome of the Rock. This important shrine is one of the holy places of Islam that would prove an obstacle to most kinds of archaeological investigation.[12] However, from the biblical texts, other descriptions and similar temple remains found elsewhere, we have a fairly good idea of what the original design was like.

The temple was oriented to the rising sun in the east. Its outer, rectangular courtyard allowed for the wider activities of the priests, including sacrificial offerings. The temple itself was a two-room structure following the plan of the tabernacle. The Holy of Holies enclosed what remained of the peak of Mount Moriah. The rocky outcrop remains the central feature inside the Dome of the Rock. It was here that the priest offered the blood of the sacrifice on the Day of Atonement.

The Islamic Dome of the Rock, a shrine located on the site of the temple.

One unusual architectural feature is that the pillars described at the entrance seem to have been freestanding. The interior of the temple itself was probably the largest internal space, unsupported by pillars, that could have been constructed in the ancient world. It would have been a dark and mysterious chamber, lit by the seven lights of the menorah candles.

Comparable temples excavated elsewhere may have been smaller in scale, but followed the same blueprint. Like the tabernacle, they indicate that the ancient world understood this convention. The temple was a place where a god could dwell among his people and rule them. However, the unique feature of the Israelite temple was found in the contents of the Holy Place. Instead of Pharaoh sitting on his throne or a statue to a deity in the Holy Place, the Israelites housed God's Word in the ark of the covenant.[13] God would not dwell among his people through a person or an idol, but through his covenant Word. The temple was demolished and rebuilt, and then refurbished on such a scale by the time of Jesus that very little of Solomon's original construction remained. However, the Word of God and his covenant remained central to God's people, and that would continue without the temple of stone.

Jesus and the temple

Jesus himself draws attention to this great significance of the temple. John describes God as 'tabernacling' on earth in Jesus (John 1:14).[14] When his critics question his authority to drive out the merchants from the temple courts, Jesus replies, 'Destroy this temple, and I will raise it again in three days' (John 2:19). His claim would be used against him in his trial and execution (Matthew 26:61; 27:40). The temple Jesus was speaking of was built, not of stone, but of his own body. After the destruction of his life by crucifixion, Jesus was raised from the dead three days later.

The historic tabernacle and temple are now understood as pictures for the reality of what Christ came to do. When he died on the cross, he fulfilled the function of sacrifice in bringing us forgiveness before a holy God. At his death, the curtain of the temple was torn in two (Luke 23:45). N. T. Wright explains, 'With Jesus' resurrection, judgement has been passed on the Temple, and . . . Jesus himself is now the place where, and the means by which, the [F]ather's presence and forgiving love are to be known.'[15] Without the Old Testament temple worship, we would not be prepared to understand the full significance of what Christ came to do. Now that he has come, we can understand what it means for him to bring forgiveness of sin and a restored relationship to God. The church, as the body of Christ, is described as the temple in the New Testament.[16] This is not a reference to later church and chapel buildings. Christian believers, joined together through the gospel, become the place where God dwells and brings people to himself.

Even as time travellers to ancient Israel, we would not be able to gain access to the temple. Only the priests had that privilege. But the significance of the temple is now found in a relationship to God through Christ, accessible to anyone and everyone to the very ends of the earth.

Bible field trip

Reading: Isaiah 46:1–13
Date: 740 BC
Destination: Jerusalem

1. Bel and Nebo are two of Babylon's primary gods. What is going to happen to them (verses 1–2)?

2. Contrast what the Lord does for his people with these idols (verses 1–4).

3. How are idols made (verses 5–7)?

4. What is God going to do for his people (verses 8–13)? To find out who the 'bird of prey' is, see Isaiah 45:1 and Ezra 1:1–2.

7

LAYING DOWN THE LAW

Did you know that, by 1800, there were 200 crimes in England that warranted the death penalty? Forgery, stealing horses, pilfering more than 25p from a shop, damaging Westminster Bridge in London and impersonating a pensioner could all be punishable by death. Still on the statute are laws that prevent a Member of Parliament from entering the House of Commons wearing a full suit of armour, and requiring any Royal Navy ship calling into London to present the port authority with a barrel of rum. Of course, many of these laws are repealed as time passes. The law forbidding eating mince pies on Christmas Day was only in force from 1647 to 1680, when our appetites got the better of us. However, the law that required London cab drivers to carry a bale of hay on every trip was only repealed in 1976, long after ponies had ceased to power their vehicles.

Visiting Israel even today, the traveller is confronted with many confusing regulations and restrictions. Knowing what clothing is acceptable when visiting a holy site and why milk is unavailable in a restaurant can be very helpful. But as we visit ancient Israel, we encounter religious and social laws that seem even more alien to us. Who cares how crops are sown or what fabrics are used in clothing, and what on earth is the problem with eating bacon? However, the law is very important in the Old Testament, and so we need to suspend our prejudices for a moment and think about why laws mattered so much and what kind of society God was creating at that time.

Laying down the law

Christians have very different attitudes to the law given through Moses. Some believe that these laws are still very much in force and that we should reconstruct modern society along the same lines. This is difficult, because everyone ends up picking and choosing, for one reason or another. We don't apply the laws that are related to sacrifice, because Jesus has fulfilled the purpose of animal sacrifice, and we don't keep the same food laws, because we believe they represented a barrier between Jew and Gentile that is no longer in force. So why do we pick some but not others?

Many Christians have taught that there are different kinds of laws in the Old Testament, some universal that still apply, and others temporary that only applied in ancient Israel. This approach often divides the law into three different types. John Calvin, the Reformer, described these as moral, ceremonial and civil. The moral laws, like not stealing, are those governing our personal behaviour. The ceremonial laws concern sacrifice and worship. The civil laws are those which provide order and government for society. Something along these lines can be found throughout church history. The great Roman Catholic theologian, Thomas Aquinas, wrote,

> We must therefore distinguish three kinds of precept in the Old Law; viz. 'moral' precepts, which are dictated by the natural law; 'ceremonial' precepts, which are determinations of the Divine worship; and 'judicial' precepts, which are determinations of the justice to be maintained among men.[1]

The threefold division of the law can be helpful when we read the Old Testament and apply moral teachings in our own day. The Ten Commandments are moral laws binding on our personal life. The ceremonial laws governing what is clean and unclean are no longer binding upon us, as we worship through the purity of Christ (Hebrews 9:10–14). The judicial laws helped to govern ancient Israel and order society. As we are no longer an ancient agrarian culture, we cannot expect these laws to have the same relevance to us today.

The idea that some of the laws are more important than others should not surprise us. The prophets of the Old Testament recognized this (Hosea 6:6), and Jesus shared this prophetic understanding with his denunciation of the Pharisees: 'Woe to you, teachers of the law and Pharisees, you hypocrites! You give a tenth of your spices—mint, dill and cumin. But you have neglected the more important matters of the law—justice, mercy and faithfulness' (Matthew 23:23). Jesus affirms the value of even the details of the law, like offering a tithe, but still distinguishes the 'more important matters'. Not all laws are equally important.

However, many theologians find the threefold division artificial. The Bible itself does not present the law this way. In fact, far from it, the law is presented as an organic whole. It is very difficult to start disentangling different types of law from each other. For example, the Ten Commandments are generally understood to be moral law, but attitudes to the Sabbath still vary. Should it be celebrated on Saturday or

Sunday? And why do we not continue to impose the same restrictions on our behaviour today as they did in the Old Testament era? Orthodox Jews certainly try to do so, with various Sabbath regulations regarding the use of elevators, kitchens and electronic gadgets. Christians keep the Sabbath in a way far removed from the practice of Orthodox Jews. Therefore, even in teaching which might be the clearest example of the moral law, there is a difficulty in application.

It seems odd to describe some laws as moral. We would never want to imply that the other laws were 'immoral'! Surely all laws are moral, but their moral teaching may apply in different ways. Many theologians are drawn towards an interpretation of the law that takes into account the underlying reasons why the law was given.

Understanding Torah

The Hebrew word 'Torah' is done a disservice when translated into English as 'law'. Our English word implies a list of rules and a concern with keeping out of trouble. You could be a nasty person, but still keep on the right side of the law! *Torah* is a much richer Hebrew word than our modern English use of *law* would imply. A possible root word means to shoot or throw, and it really indicates direction rather than simply rules. Torah provides a way of life that will lead to peace, prosperity and a living relationship with God. This is why the Old Testament is full of delight in Torah (Psalms 1:2; 119:18, 72). The ancient Israelites found pleasure in Torah, and they celebrated God's law.

The Torah was not a system of merit in order for Israelites to gain access to a blessed afterlife. It was after their redemption from Egypt as slaves that God gave them the Torah. Alec Motyer draws attention to the importance of this sequence:

'We see that what the Lord does precedes what the Lord demands, as the work of redemption prepares for the promulgation of the law.'[2] God was calling his people to enter a new land marked not just by geographical boundaries, but also by ethical boundaries. They were the people of God, and now this was what the people of God were to look like. Obedience follows grace. Having been rescued from Egypt, they had been given a blueprint for life. God's rescued people should start resembling the one who had rescued them!

We might ask, why these particular laws? Why behave in this particular way and not some other way? Torah is given by God, so that the Israelites may 'walk in all his ways' (see Micah 6:8). Old Testament scholar Christopher Wright underlines the profound implications of this. Torah reflects the character of God, so for Israel, 'in a sense their own history was an "incarnation" of the LORD, for in it he expressly revealed his own identity, character and ethical values'.[3] Torah enabled the Israelites to reflect God's character in that time and place. They should be holy, as their God is holy (Leviticus 19:2).

We are not an ancient Iron Age culture living on farms without modern technology. So there are many laws that will not apply directly to us, and many situations that those laws will not directly address. Nor are we a people living before the coming of Christ and ignorant of the new stage in salvation history brought by him. For reasons like these, we cannot simply lift the Torah from the world of ancient Israel and apply it directly to the modern world. But the values it speaks of remain eternal and continue to reveal to us the character of God and the values he requires of us.

Christopher Wright provides a convincing description of the way law functions as a paradigm. A paradigm is a pattern or model that we can learn from in order to apply the same essential ethics in our own context: 'Israel as a society was intended from the start to be a paradigm or model to the nations, a showcase of the way God longs for human society as a whole to operate.'[4] A modern nation cannot be ancient Israel, for a number of theological and historical reasons. But the same God calls people to walk in his ways. The Old Testament law provides the grammar to know what kind of lives we should be constructing.

In certain respects, the traditional threefold approach to the law and the understanding of law as paradigm are not poles apart. Some laws will be easier to apply than others. The laws not to steal or murder may be relatively straightforward to apply in our own time and place; their moral force is obvious. But the laws governing clothing or diet can seem entirely alien and inapplicable. They speak of Israel's distinctiveness from other nations. In that sense, they will no longer apply directly to the church. But we will still learn from them. Torah provides a model of what God is looking for, from which we can continue to learn.

You are what you eat

Those of us who love a bacon sandwich are immediately confronted with a dilemma. Why are some animals clean to eat and others unclean? Some Christians even believe that these dietary restrictions should remain in force for them, so they avoid prawn cocktails and bacon double cheeseburgers.[5] Are they correct?

The church has generally understood that these dietary requirements came to an end with the teaching of Jesus. He declared 'all foods clean' (Mark 7:19), and in a vision, Peter was commanded to eat unclean animals, with the warning: 'Do not call anything impure that God has made clean' (Acts

10:15). Paul warned the early church against groups that would try to impose certain food laws on them (1 Timothy 4:3). However, even if we are comfortable with the idea that we can now enjoy a crocodile steak (high in protein, low in fat, by the way), why were these laws given in the first place, and in what way do we learn from them as a paradigm for us?

Descriptions of which animals are clean and therefore edible are found in Leviticus 11 and Deuteronomy 14. Clean land animals were those that had a split hoof and chewed the cud (ox good, camel bad); water creatures were those that had fins and scales (cod good, crab bad); and insects were those that had wings but leaped (locusts good, beetles bad). As for birds, the law provides a list of those to be avoided, but the reason for others being clean to eat is not given, other than their not appearing on the unclean list. Most of the unclean birds are carrion eating—like the vulture and hawk—but not all.

The ancient Israelites really did keep these laws. Archaeological digs in Israel carefully record the bones that are found on site. The absence of pig bones is a clear indication of an Israelite settlement, while their presence points to non-Israelite occupation. But why did God make this restriction?

The simplest explanation for the food law is that it relates to hygiene. Many of the unclean animals are scavengers, and some have digestive systems that do little to deal with dangerous bacteria. Clean animals tend to be those that are less likely to transmit disease. So it could simply be for health reasons that the Israelites were to avoid certain foods. This is a reason why some health advisors continue to believe that the Old Testament food laws have a practical application today.

Other Christians believe that the food laws are quite arbitrary. It does not matter greatly which foods are clean or unclean. If God declares them so for the ancient Israelites, then this is a test of their obedience. These laws enabled the Israelites to declare their distinctive identity. It was a public, visible statement of their commitment to Yahweh in a pagan world. And this would also help explain why the dietary restrictions came to an end with the birth of the church.

Food laws, clothing and the practice of circumcision were like badges for the Israelites. They were unique and distinct from the rest of the world. These badges were continual reminders to themselves and to those who watched that they were to be a light in the darkness. Since the coming of Jesus, such boundary markers are deliberately broken down. In Christ, there is no longer Jew and Gentile, for we are all one in Christ (Galatians 3:28). This would explain why God gave Peter the vision of unclean animals to eat, prior to his meeting with pagan Cornelius. It had been important to separate Jew from Gentile, but now it was important to unite them.

If the dietary laws are primarily boundary markers, then in what sense do they continue to apply to a lobster-eating Christian today? Consider again the point of these laws: 'Do not defile yourselves by any animal or bird or anything that moves along the ground. . . . You are to be holy to me because I, the LORD, am holy, and I have set you apart from the nations to be my own' (Leviticus 20:25–26). The laws distinguish between being defiled and being holy. Being 'holy' means to be set apart as God's distinctive people. To be 'defiled' would be to mix faith with worldliness and thereby lose distinctiveness. The Israelites 'were to reflect that separateness in every aspect of their daily lives—in their food and clothing and in their conduct'.[6] The Christian continues to be called to a life of holiness. Paul calls the Corinthians to 'touch no unclean thing'. This no longer means animal carcasses, but avoiding 'everything that contaminates body and spirit', so that they may perfect 'holiness out of reverence for God'

(2 Corinthians 6:17; 7:1). The Israelite avoidance of certain foods made visible their commitment to Yahweh. What makes our commitment to Christ visible to a watching world today?

Marriage

Men and women were normally married. The Old Testament tells us a lot less about the legal issues surrounding marriage than we might expect. We know that, by New Testament times, the minimum age for a girl to marry was twelve, but the law does not actually specify this. We know some Old Testament kings married at the age of fourteen, so it is safe to assume it was not unusual for people to marry in their teenage years. Parents could arrange marriages, but this was not necessarily without the consent of the young people involved. Even in the ancient patriarchal story of Abraham arranging for a girl to marry his son Isaac, we read that her permission was sought (Genesis 24:57–58).

Marriage involved a formal business contract. This did not mean that women were treated as objects, or that love was not involved (Genesis 24:67). But in the harsh reality of the ancient world, financial exchanges did help to ensure security. The man would pay a bride price to the girl's parents as a kind of compensation for their loss of a family member who would otherwise be working. We do not know what form the marriage ceremony may have taken, but an exchange of gifts ensured that the marriage was a publicly recognized contract between two people, rather than simply a private expression of love.

The ideal of marriage is laid down in creation: 'a man leaves his father and mother and is united to his wife, and they become one flesh' (Genesis 2:24). But the legal code of the Old Testament deals with the harsh complexities of a fallen world. The law prohibited sex outside the marriage contract. The practice of polygamy began with Lamech (Genesis 4:19), and many significant Old Testament characters had more than one wife. Stories that describe men married to more than one wife regularly show it to be a cause of problems. Abraham and Elkanah both provoke rivalry among their multiple partners (Genesis 16:5; 1 Samuel 1:7). So what was permissible was certainly not necessarily desirable.

Similarly, the Old Testament law did not approve the practice of divorce, but rather recognized and regulated it. Divorce was possible on certain grounds. The law prevented a woman from being dismissed by a man and then taken back like an object (Deuteronomy 24:1–4). In fact, the purpose of the law of divorce was to protect the woman. Having been given a 'certificate' of divorce, she was released from the marriage contract and free to remarry. If she could not remarry, she might face poverty. Remarriage after bereavement was particularly important, and the law laid a principle of duty on the brother of the deceased to take in the widow as a wife (Leviticus 25:25). This law provides the background to events in the book of Ruth. Without such a 'kinsman redeemer', the widow might die destitute.

So are divorce and remarriage acceptable? We have to remember that the law made provisions for a fallen people in a fallen world. As a reflection of God's standards, such laws demonstrate both his holy standards and his mercy. Divorce could protect a neglected wife, and polygamy could provide for a destitute woman. God is on the side of the 'widow and orphan' in the law. Commenting on the provision of divorce, Jesus said, 'It was because your hearts were hard that Moses wrote you this law' (Mark 10:5), and he points further back to creation, where God's ideal of a man and woman in an unbreakable bond is clearly established.

Sex was for a man and woman within the marriage bond; anything else was either adultery or a misuse of the sexual act (Leviticus 18). It is important to notice how unusual many of these sexual prohibitions were in the context of Israel's neighbours. For example, there are no parallel prohibitions on sex between men in other ancient cultures. It was practised and approved of in ancient Egypt, Babylon, Assyria and the classical cultures of Greece and Rome. Gordon Wenham, surveying the literature across the ancient world, concludes, 'The Old Testament rejection of all kinds of homosexual practice is apparently unique in the ancient world.'[7] Only when Christianity came to influence the highest levels of Roman society did such practices become unacceptable to the wider world.

An obvious question regarding the laws on sexual purity is whether they belong with the dietary laws, as examples of ritual boundary markers, no longer relevant to today's church. Such an argument is difficult to sustain. The sexual laws guard the original creation provision for marriage between a man and a woman (Genesis 2:24). The other forms of sexual practice described (including bestiality, incest and rape) all go against God's original creation mandate. For that reason, Paul describes such practices as 'unnatural' (Romans 1:26). What is natural cannot be defined by contemporary society, only by God's original creation. With regard to homosexuality, it is also worth pointing out that the Old Testament laws concern the sexual act itself, but indicate nothing about what is sometimes called 'sexual orientation'. There is no evidence that the ancient Israelites thought in such terms.

The Year of Jubilee

The law had a great deal to say about how wealth was managed. The emphasis was upon responsibility to the wider community, rather than preservation of personal wealth. While theft was certainly against the law, so too was the failure to provide for the poor and needy. The tribal allotment of the land of Canaan is particularly instructive.

When the Israelites entered Canaan, they were given land in proportion to the size of their tribe (Numbers 26:52–56). But it was not a commodity to be bought and sold and enlarged, to the detriment of other people. Every fifty years there was a Jubilee year in which all land returned to the original owners (Leviticus 25). This would rule out the possibility of a 'landed' class developing. No one could gradually amass more and more of the land, pushing fellow Israelites into the status of serfs without land. When land was bought and sold, its price was set against the remaining years before the Jubilee. In effect, the Israelites were tenants. They only possessed land on trust from God. It was not an absolute possession.

Providing for all

Because land was so important for farming and survival, the law made special provision for widows, orphans and refugees (Deuteronomy 14:28–29). The care of Israelites for the poor and vulnerable would enable everyone to celebrate in God's kindness. When the landless are provided for, 'Then you and the Levites and the foreigners residing among you shall rejoice in all the good things the LORD your God has given to you and your household' (Deuteronomy 26:11).

The Sabbath rest was not only for the ancient Israelites one day in seven, but also a principle of rest for the land. One year in seven, the land itself should remain fallow. This is of proven agricultural value, and until the development of modern technologies, the practice continued until recent times. The land could recover and restore its nutrients. However, there is a further detail in the Old Testament law that provides another insight into the character of God. Land left fallow would allow wild animals to benefit. They could live and eat in these untended areas (Exodus 23:11). Likewise, in the weekly Sabbath, the working animals were given rest for the day (Exodus 23:12). God is always interested in his animal creation (Mark 1:13; Matthew 6:26).

The Old Testament laws regarding the land, along with prohibitions on charging interest, all point to a strong sense of equality. Just as land reverted to original owners in the Year of Jubilee, debts among Israelites were cancelled every seven years. These laws would continually self-correct the human instinct to amass wealth. In modern society, our economic system can favour inequalities. It is easier for the rich to get richer than for the poor to climb out of their poverty. Wealth generates wealth; poverty becomes a trap. In contrast, the ancient Israelites had laws that made fresh starts possible and prevented a few individuals from monopolizing resources. Or, at least, that was the ideal.

Harsh reality

The reality of ancient Israel is that many of these laws were probably not put into practice. There is little evidence, either from Scripture or from outside the Bible, that the Israelites held the Year of Jubilee. This might not surprise us. The wealthy and prosperous were unlikely to press for its implementation; the poor and vulnerable were in no position to demand their rights. However, God cannot be mocked. He had his own way of ensuring his will was done. In 2 Chronicles 36:21, the land is described as enjoying 'its sabbath rests' during the seventy years that Judah was in exile. Perhaps the seventy years of exile were related to seventy missing Jubilee years? That would equate to 490 years in which the Jubilee had not been held. During those seventy years of exile, the 'poorest people of the land' would work the vineyards and fields (2 Kings 25:12), and Ezekiel was given a vision of 'wild animals' ruling the land (Ezekiel 33:27). God ensured that the Jubilee was practised, even without willing Israelites.

Policing the law

It is one thing to have laws, but another to be able to enforce them. As a time traveller to ancient Israel, you would have seen military soldiers, but noticed the absence of a police force. So what did the ancient Israelites do without police and prisons?

The primary responsibility for teaching and enforcing the law lay within the family. Parents had a duty to teach the law to their children and to ensure they lived in the way of their Lord. In ancient Israel, there were no formal synagogues or rabbis. The priesthood took care of the sacrificial system either at the temple or at smaller shrines, but it was for the father to teach his family Torah. Beyond the family lay a gathering of men called the elders. Quite how they were selected is unclear, but they would have been a number of respected fathers, functioning together as judges for their community.

Under the monarchy, the king himself would have been the ultimate judge in disputes. Solomon asked for wisdom from God, and his gifting is put to the test by a complaint between two prostitutes (1 Kings 3:16–28). In this famous story, the two women had children, but one of those children had died. Solomon had to decide who was the natural mother of the surviving child. King Solomon suggests cutting the surviving child in two with a sword, so that each could have a half. The threat is merely a ploy to reveal the true nature of the two women. The mother whose child had died earlier spitefully encourages the barbaric act. The true mother pleads for the child's life, preferring to renounce her claim rather than see her child die. This story provides a memorable picture of Solomon's wisdom. But presumably, the king heard only a tiny number of cases, and few legal issues would have climbed so high up the judicial system.

Local elders dealt with most legal issues. Family lay at the heart of society, which explains why the extended family was so important to Israel. Without strong bonds of family loyalty and respect, anarchy would have reigned. In some parts of the world today, these strong bonds remain in force, and the pronouncements of a father or mother carry greater weight than those of any police officer or magistrate. But in contemporary north-west European and American culture, these bonds are fast disappearing. From our impoverished point of view, we find it hard to imagine life without a professional police force.

Crime and punishment

Ancient Israel had no real prison system. However, this was not unusual in the ancient world, where prisons would have been expensive to run. But kings had their dungeons. The Egyptian pharaoh threw Joseph into one, just as Joseph would in turn have his own brothers locked up for a time. The king of Babylon imprisoned King Zedekiah, and Jeremiah was lowered into a cistern. The Romans did use prison cells, and so, by the time of the New Testament, we find parables concerning prison, and the apostles spending time behind bars.

Among the ancient Israelites, there were some improvised means of custody (Leviticus 24:12; Number 15:34). But this was probably just a way of holding lawbreakers, while elders decided what to do with them. When it came to judgment, the penalties were some kind of compensation or the death penalty.

Fines were often in the form of payments to the offended party as a matter of compensation for a wrong done. However, it was common practice to take matters into one's own hands and return violence for violence. The Old Testament law sought to control such behaviour. 'An eye for an eye and a tooth for a tooth' (see Exodus 21:24) is interesting in this regard. Such an expression is not unique to the Bible, also appearing in Babylonian legal codes. It acts as a restraint on retribution. The offended party cannot go further than the crime committed and cannot take vengeance on other family members. Later, Jewish rabbis interpreted this law as metaphorical. The law provides a guide for what kind of financial compensation would be appropriate, rather than commending literal, bodily mutilation. However, what is unique to the Old Testament example is that this law applies to all people, irrespective of class. In the Babylonian law code, the principle applies only to those of the same class in society. The Old Testament law persistently points towards equality.

The death penalty

The crimes for which the death penalty was appropriate signify the gravity of these offences. Unlike surrounding nations, the death penalty was not imposed for theft or property issues. People matter more than possessions, and this is reflected in the implementation of such a penalty.

Capital punishment was for murder; sexual crimes, including rape; worshipping other gods; and human trafficking. Treating people as possessions or dabbling in occult practices were clearly held up as the worst crimes. However, the law even authorized the death penalty for rebellious sons (Deuteronomy 21:18–21), something worth further consideration.

The law says that, if a son is stubborn and rebellious, unwilling to obey his parents, then they are to bring him before the community elders. If the elders accept the charges, then the community is to execute the son. Harsh? Certainly. But consider the context. The son is not a child; he is described as a 'drunkard'. His refusal to obey his parents undermines the very heart of ancient Israel's government. Remember, it is family that teaches and enforces the law. Without family authority, there is no government. But the parents cannot do anything themselves—that would be murder. The charges must be made public, at the town gate, and brought before an outside body of leaders. Only they can adjudicate. This process highlights the importance of preserving family authority, but it also provides a check against parental abuse. We have to wonder if this law ever actually had to be enforced. Even for the most dysfunctional families, the loss of a son would have been an economic hit. And even for the most stubborn of sons, the long walk to the town gate may have been enough to bring about a change of heart.

Many people are disturbed by the presence of the death penalty in the Old Testament. However, we should remember its context. A prison system was not economically viable, and the most serious crimes had to be met with the most serious punishments, in order to prevent society from breaking down. Before we throw stones, perhaps we need to respect just how well ancient societies managed to achieve cohesion and security without policing and prisons. Harsh penalties were part of the culture. The possibility of a community living without fear of murder and abuse was the gain.

Raising the bar

The Old Testament law remains of abiding relevance to the modern world and the Christian life. This is not because we seek to apply it in a crude or literal sense. We are not ancient Israel, and we do not live in their kind of society. We do not need laws to regulate slavery or polygamy, because earlier generations of Christians succeeded in abolishing those practices altogether.[8]

Jesus spoke authoritatively of the continuing significance of the Old Testament law: 'Do not think that I have come to abolish the Law or the Prophets; I have not come to abolish them but to fulfil them' (Matthew 5:17). What did he mean? Certainly, in his death and resurrection, he brought to fulfilment the sacrificial and ceremonial purpose of the law. Who would want to sacrifice a lamb or a pigeon, now that Jesus Christ has given his own priceless life on our behalf? It is not that the ancient Israelites were wrong to practise their ceremonial system. In their day it was correct. But that system is no longer required.

But what of the moral and ethical instructions of the law? Some Christians give the impression that the ancient Israelites were under law, while we are under grace and can now lighten up. The God of judgment has gone; we now worship the God of grace. But this is a misunderstanding.

Jesus actually said, 'Unless your righteousness surpasses that of the Pharisees and the teachers of the law, you will certainly not enter the kingdom of heaven' (Matthew 5:20). How can our righteousness surpass theirs? Jesus provides an answer in the Sermon on the Mount. In this extended treatment of the Old Testament law, Jesus never tells us to do less than ancient Israel. He tells us to do more.

The demands of Jesus are higher, not lower, than those of Moses. The Old Testament said do not murder; Jesus tells us not to lose our temper. The Old Testament said do not commit adultery; Jesus tells us not to indulge lust. The fact that we may work towards a more tolerant, generous public society does not mean we tolerate sin in our own hearts.

Torah pointed to the character of God. In a simple, pictorial way, ancient Israel provided an illustration of the holiness of God. Now, in Christ, our eyes have been raised higher still. Like Torah, we follow the law of Christ, to show greater love to our neighbours and ever greater love to God. The ultimate demand of Jesus is not that we keep out of prison, but that we 'be perfect, therefore, as [our] heavenly Father is perfect' (Matthew 5:48). In this high calling, ancient Israel's law provides many lessons and many warnings.

Bible field trip

Reading: Exodus 20:1–21
Date: c.1400 BC
Destination: The Sinai Desert

1. How does God describe himself (verses 1–7)?

2. Taking the commands as a whole, how would we summarize God's priorities (verses 2–17)?

3. Why are we given a command to rest on the Sabbath, and how does this apply to us today (verses 8–11)?

4. How do the people respond to what they see (verses 18–21)? Should this be a lesson to us today?

8

WAR AND PEACE

In September 1938, the British Prime Minister, Neville Chamberlain, touched down at Heston Aerodrome in England, fresh from diplomatic meetings with Germany's Nazi government. Waving a piece of paper in the air, he announced a peace treaty for Europe, bearing the signature of Adolf Hitler, which he declared to represent 'peace for our time'. That memorable night he gave a further speech, concluding, 'Go home and get a nice quiet sleep.' The following morning, Germany occupied the Sudetenland, and Hitler's military ambitions continued unabated. The Second World War would commence within a year. In the context of world history, warfare has seemed to be a common thread, and so we should not be surprised to meet it regularly in Scripture too.

Israel was born in turbulent times. To whatever point in her history you wish to journey, war will not be very far away. Be prepared to encounter great armies and lethal weapons, because there never was an easy peace in ancient Israel. We are about to see both war and peace, but we begin with Israel's escape from one of the most technologically advanced military powers of the time.

Out of Egypt

The Israelites were unarmed slave labourers in Egypt. However, it is often pointed out, as we have seen already, that slave labour was not used to build the famous pyramids. That is entirely true, but the pyramids have nothing to do with the exodus story. By the time of Moses, they are already ancient history. The Israelites are being used to build grain storage facilities. In ever harder conditions, they will make the mud bricks to be used in public building works, bricks fired in ovens to make them very strong. The work was back-breaking, allowing for no respite. The Egyptians treated them badly. One reason for this was that they were never considered native Egyptians. Even though they had been living in the land for 400 years, their appearance and culture were different. They were settlers from Canaan and, therefore, always considered immigrants.

The conditions in which the Israelites laboured resulted partly from the fear their rapid population growth inspired in the Egyptian government (Exodus 1:7). A large immigrant population posed a risk to nationalists: 'If war breaks out, [they] will join our enemies, fight against us and leave the country' (Exodus 1:10). So the Egyptian policy was to work the Israelites hard and attempt to exterminate their baby boys.

The Bible records a number of place names in relation to the exodus, but many of them can no longer be identified. This reflects many changes in the topography of the region due to shifting sands and water courses.

Goshen was a district in the north-east corner of Egypt. Here the Israelites became numerous. One of the cities that they built, Rameses, has been identified at modern-day Qantir, and archaeological remains confirm the presence of foreign settlers.

The great escape

After the devastating tenth plague on Egypt, the Israelites begin their march towards the Promised Land. The obvious route to Canaan was along a major coastal thoroughfare, the Way of the Philistines. The walk would have taken less than a month. However, the coastal route had a major obstacle. The Egyptians called this same road 'The Way of Horus' and built a number of fortresses along it. This explains God's strategy in directing the Israelites south: 'God did not lead them on the road through the Philistine country, though that was shorter. For God said, "If they face war, they might change their minds and return to Egypt"' (Exodus 13:17). This may seem odd—after all, the Israelites would face war in any case when they entered Canaan. But God knew he had to prepare them for this. A direct confrontation with the Egyptian military in an area where Egypt would have had the upper hand was not what he wanted for them. So instead, God led them south towards the Red Sea. Yet, in a dramatic twist and in hot pursuit came a pharaoh who had changed his mind, with 600 of his finest war chariots. After all, a massive loss of slave labour could seriously damage the Egyptian economy. Here God would deliver the Israelites not through conflict, but the miraculous parting of the Red Sea.

Which Red Sea?

We call the sea that the Israelites crossed the Red Sea by tradition, not translation. The Hebrew name is the Sea of

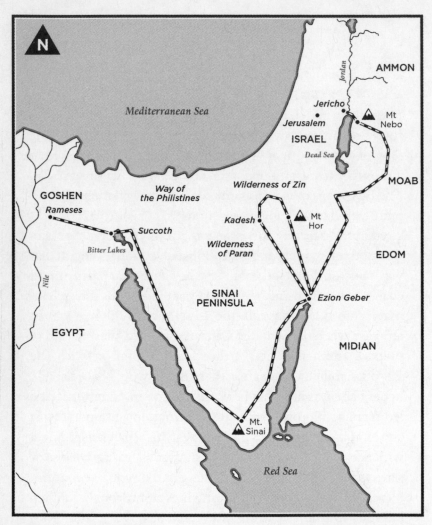

MAP OF THE EXODUS

Reeds.[1] But when the Hebrew Old Testament was translated into Greek, the Red Sea was better known, and so this Greek name was used. In fact, what we call the Red Sea today could be called the Sea of Reeds (1 Kings 9:26). When the Greek-speaking Christians described the events of the exodus, their use of the name Red Sea had become established (Acts 7:36). But Red Sea may simply be a loose reference to all the waters south and west of the Sinai desert. However, many Christians continue to believe that the crossing point was somewhere in the present-day Red Sea, even though there are serious problems with the proposed archaeological evidence for this.

The location of the Sea of Reeds is hinted at during the plagues on Egypt. After the plague of locusts, we read that the Lord provided a strong west wind that blew all their carcasses into the Sea of Reeds (Exodus 10:19). This was a plague of locusts, so thick that the Bible says the ground had been covered until it was black. So how far did the west wind blow all those billions of locust carcasses? If they were blown into what we call the Red Sea, that means a journey of 800 miles across the Sinai Peninsula. The Bible implies that the sea is closer to hand.

On the shore of the Sea of Reeds, the escaping Israelites are literally trapped. The Egyptian army is bearing down on them. Desert is all around. The north-east coastal road is studded with Egyptian forts. And an impassable sea lies before them. Only a divine miracle can make their escape possible. Moses encourages his people with the words: 'The LORD will fight for you; you need only to be still' (Exodus 14:14). That sounds very spiritual, but in fact, Moses was not entirely correct! God says to him, 'Why are you crying out to me? Tell the Israelites to move on.' Being still was not in fact God's solution. The Israelites were called to march ahead, towards the barrier of the sea.

God sends a wind from the east. (If the locusts were still being blown towards the modern-day Red Sea, that would have brought them back!) This wind divides the water and allows them to pass through, as if between walls. This image reminds us that the Sea of Reeds was not just a patch of marshy ground. Though the lakes have come and gone over the years with the changing Egyptian topography, the Bitter Lakes still there today are deep enough to provide a formidable obstacle to any body of travellers.[2]

The traditional site of Mount Sinai is Jebel Musa, in the south of the Sinai Peninsula. From here, the Israelites had a direct march north into Canaan. However, their own stubbornness led to a forty-year delay, before another generation of Israelites would actually set foot in the Promised Land. During these years, they were not wandering around lost. Like modern-day Bedouin, they would have lived a nomadic lifestyle, camped in the Sinai, before entering the land.

Conquest

A fixed point for the entry of the Israelites into the land of Canaan is 1203 BC, at which time the people were being referred to on an Egyptian commemorative inscription. Pharaoh Merneptah (reigned 1213–1203 BC) carried out a military campaign in the region. He refers to the suppression of various Canaanite cities. In the list is also the first direct reference outside the Bible to the people of Israel. Archaeological evidence confirms an influx of settlers during the thirteenth century BC.

So the most straightforward route into the land would have been from the south, but instead, Joshua leads the Israelites along the eastern edge of the region and then crosses the Jordan to enable entry into the land at a midway point. Jericho is the first Canaanite city that is conquered. Looking at our map, we see this makes enormous strategic sense. Rather than working gradually north, facing ever-increasing opposition from city states that might unify before them, Joshua splits the region in two and is able to conquer the southern region (Joshua 6), before turning north (Joshua 11).

Three cities are described as being destroyed by fire: Ai, Hazor and Jericho. Of the three, only Hazor has been subject to significant contemporary archaeological work. It was the largest and best-fortified city in the region at that time. But excavations have revealed its destruction by fire some time during the Late Bronze Age. The fire was so hot that worked stone in public buildings actually cracked. Among the charred remains, statues of gods were found to have been deliberately broken. While it is not possible to prove that this is the work of Joshua, the evidence is certainly in keeping with what we read in the Bible.

Settlers of Canaan

The destruction of cities was limited and not really God's plan for the conquest. As we have already seen, God was using the

Building stones from Hazor, cracked in 1300°C heat (3272°F).

Israelites to fulfil a promise to judge the people of the region for their sin (Genesis 15:16). But the conquest also provided homes, land and resources to the recently freed slaves. It was not God's intention to wipe out the region and start all over again. Therefore, the archaeological record at this point should not be expected to show enormous discontinuities. The Israelites merely took over cities and houses, continuing to farm fields and harvest from vines. The conquest enlarged the population of Canaan, but it did not lead to a radical discontinuity in culture or settlements.

How many people lived in Canaan? Detailed population studies of the ancient world have been carried out, offering us more than tentative conclusions.

A population can be estimated on the basis of the density in which people could realistically live, given accommodation and available resources. In a simple settlement, an approximate measure might be 250 people per hectare. Of course, in practice, things are more complicated. Houses could have two or three storeys for living space above, and large public buildings can reduce the area for occupation. So a major city could have a lower density than a smaller town, simply because valuable space is taken up by public buildings like temples or palaces.

A more accurate measure of population concentrates on the number of household dwellings. However, this method assumes that all have been identified, and that an accurate estimate can be made about the average size of an ancient family. This may all sound like mere guesswork, but it does provide some parameters. A settlement would house somewhere between 200 and 500 people per hectare, depending on local conditions.

This means that the population of Canaan, prior to the arrival of the Israelites, is estimated to have been in the region of 140,000. During ancient Israel's Iron Age the population grew to about 400,000. Taking a single city, Jerusalem, estimates suggest a population of 2,000 at the time of King David, and 20,000 by the time of King Josiah. The highest figure for the region is in the wake of the Roman occupation, when the population may even have reached one million.[3]

These figures give rise to a problem. How many Israelites left Egypt and entered the land? The Bible records 603,550 men of fighting age (Numbers 1:46) leaving Egypt, and 601,730 entering the land (Numbers 26:51). During the time of King David, a census numbers the adult men at 1.3 million (2 Samuel 24:9). When we add women and children to the list, we have a number of Israelites ranging from 2 to 5 million strong. In the modern world, such numbers pose no problem, but in the ancient world such numbers are unheard of, and difficult to square with the archaeological record.

There is no doubt that the Israelites were vast in number. In Egypt they 'became so numerous that the land was filled with them' (Exodus 1:7). But even several thousand would have been a large number in the ancient world. The entire population of Jericho at the time of the conquest was no more than 4,000, and Pharaoh sought to pursue the fleeing Israelites with 600 chariots. Just to put the numbers into perspective, we are told that when the Israelites passed through Moab, they promised the king that they would stay on the road and not set foot in the fields or vineyards (Numbers 20:17). Over 2 million people on a road of ordinary width would produce a procession over 2,000 miles in length. While the Israelite at the rear end of such a march would still be in Egypt, Moses at its head would have reached the borders of China!

There are some clues that we may be misreading the numbers in the Old Testament. There may be something about the calculations of a census that we do not understand.

For one thing, when the Israelites crossed the River Jordan to enter the Promised Land, the number given is 40,000 (Joshua 4:13). We are even told that the Israelites were fewer in number than other nations (Deuteronomy 7:7).

An alternative reading of the numbers is that the Hebrew word for 1,000 ('lp) could mean a group or fighting unit.[4] In that case, at the exodus the Israelites could deploy 603 military units of fighting men. That would explain Pharaoh's calculation of sending 600 of his finest war chariots into the pursuit. One chariot was sent per fighting troop of Israelites.

City life

The city was always key in the development of civilization in the ancient world. It would become a hub for administration, trade, culture and diplomatic relations with the wider world. Cities were virtual states, with their own kings, during the Bronze Age. After the conquest, the Israelites formed a unified kingdom under a single king.

King Saul did not look much like our image of a prestigious monarch. When he is called upon to make his first royal decision, we find him 'returning from the fields, behind his oxen' (1 Samuel 11:5). Saul is a man of the people, with his own farm to manage. Living in Gibeah, he had no palace, throne or court. However, Saul did begin to develop a standing army (1 Samuel 14:52), and his house becomes a headquarters, with attendants and a young David on hand to play the harp.

King David develops the monarchy to the next stage, by establishing a capital city. The conquest of the land under Joshua had been only a partial fulfilment. Pockets of resistance and independent Canaanite cities remained in the land. One of those cities was the ancient Jebusite town of Salem or Jebus.

Jerusalem

Jerusalem remained a Canaanite city state in the heart of the land, and it was of little economic value. In fact, it was situated up in the more mountainous territory, close to the wilderness, away from an important trade route, and it was relatively small. It would have seemed insignificant, compared to the great cities of Hazor and Megiddo. But this was the very factor that drew David to this town.

There were strategic, political reasons for David to make the city of Jebus his new capital. Because it had known no prior Israelite occupation by any of the tribes, it could function as a neutral capital. Though David was of the tribe of Judah, he had to secure the allegiance of all the tribes. Making his capital here provided a centre that could unify the nation. David was still a man of the people, a shepherd boy who had become a warrior. But having taken charge of Jebus, that was all set to change. The town was named the City of David or Jerusalem, and a palace was built (2 Samuel 5:11). The city of Jerusalem would quickly develop as the administrative and religious centre of the nation of Israel.

The idea of making Jerusalem a religious centre was clearly David's own. He relocated the ark of the covenant from the obscure town of Baalah and set up a tabernacle for it somewhere in his new city (2 Samuel 6:17). These plans were a masterstroke. David was laying down the basis for a system of government and worship that would make Jerusalem a spiritual centre for thousands of years to come.

One of David's sons, Solomon, was able to reap the reward of his father's strategy. Under King Solomon, there is a golden age of security and unity for God's people. For one brief moment in history, the Israelites are a unified people. They enjoy a level of prosperity that makes them an important player in international relations. That raises the obvious question: why is there no extrabiblical reference to Solomon from the time?

The period of King Solomon's reign reflects a window in international relations where it was possible for a relatively small nation to hold its independence with relative security. Indeed, the Bible records that Solomon entered a marriage alliance with Egypt, by marrying the daughter of Pharaoh (1 Kings 9:16). Despite protests from some modern critics that Egyptian kings did not marry their daughters to foreigners, it would have made good sense for Pharaoh Siamun, contemporary of Solomon, to make just such an alliance.[5] Having recently conquered the Philistines in the coastal strip, Pharaoh would have wanted to secure a peaceful frontier with the hill country.[6] The lack of extrabiblical references to Solomon thus far need not surprise us.

Evidence for the united monarchy of David and Solomon is most likely to emerge from Jerusalem itself. This is one of the hardest locations for archaeologists, because of the political situation. However, what has been revealed is clear confirmation of the existence of a major capital at the time of these kings. Jerusalem was not the large, lavish city we know from the time of Jesus, but a big town boasting some grand architecture. The current archaeological team working in the City of David has good reason to think that they have located the remains of a palace from the period.

It was under King Solomon that public building works developed across the region (1 Kings 9:15). A remarkable archaeological discovery of the twentieth century is a common, unique style of gate in the locations mentioned in the Bible. At Hazor, Megiddo and Gezer, a six-chambered, fortified style of stone gate complex has been unearthed. These expensive gates reflect the planning of a common architect and are located in three different tribal regions (Naphtali, Manasseh and Ephraim). Many

Reconstruction of the imposing fortified gates of Solomon's era.

archaeologists identify these as the tangible remains of Solomon's building programme. Others disagree. On the basis of the associated pottery finds, some consider the gates to belong to a period fifty or a hundred years later than the time of Solomon. However, amid the controversy, the view that these gates are the product of the unified monarchy remains credible and convincing.

Out of town

It is estimated that, during most of ancient Israel's history, 66 percent of the population lived in small villages and settlements. It is an irony that, as a city grew, it probably lost domestic dwelling space. Public building works and administrative functions took over, and so most people now lived outside the walls. They would have visited the city for worship, trade, or for reasons of safety in times of conflict.

As we've seen, rural settlements leave few traces. Farming land was valuable and not built upon, so the people would choose rocky ground for their dwellings. There would be no monumental architecture here for future generations to discover. However, those remains that have been found give us a clear picture of life in the countryside.

Many villages were arranged as a circle of houses, with a central, open courtyard, allowing for a real sense of community and extended family. This may have been the permanent version of the pattern by which they pitched their tents as nomadic people. Common house architecture also emerged among the Israelites. Dubbed the 'four-room house', it would have had a central communal space and a second storey, probably roofed in. But don't go looking for a staircase—that would be a waste of space. The only way up was by climbing a ladder. Elijah and Elisha both slept in just such attic rooms (1 Kings 17:19; 2 Kings 4:11). The flat roof itself was formed of wood and earth, strong enough to be used as additional living space. The roof was probably a cool place to relax and talk (1 Samuel 9:25), or it could have been used for storage and as a spare room. For these reasons, the law decreed that the roof should be fitted with a parapet, to prevent someone from slipping to his or her death (Deuteronomy 22:8). Health and safety has a long history!

Many animals lived on the ground floor. Sheep, goats and donkeys all shared the living space. This could have made for a very cheap and effective central heating system on cold nights! The interior would have been dark, as windows were small, with light provided by olive-oil lamps during the evening. As a visitor from the present, we would have been overwhelmed by the smell, but people growing up in such conditions would have got used to it.

Hospitality was essential for the survival of travellers. In fact, a visitor arriving in a village would have expected to be offered lodging. The Bible records angels visiting and being treated in this way (Genesis 18:3–5; Judges 6:19). The New Testament continues to recommend such customs of hospitality—after all, the lesson of the Old Testament is that you never quite know when an angel may show up (Hebrews 13:2)!

While villages had no public religious buildings, they did

have family shrines and sacred spaces. However, this practice could easily lead to idolatry. There was, for example, a man called Micah in Ephraim during the time of the Judges.[7] He decided to have an idol manufactured and placed in a domestic shrine. He appointed his son as a priest and gave him an ephod, or priestly garment, to wear. However, a wandering Levite arrived at the village. The Levites were the God-ordained priests for Israel. Micah takes him in, and he replaces his son as the priest of his domestic shrine. Perhaps Micah was trying to improve the legitimacy of his private religious site.

However, this little story is the seed of an unacceptable practice that will quickly grow in ancient Israel. Members of the tribe of Dan pass through Ephraim and meet this priest. The Danites had failed to settle the coastal strip allotted to them in the conquest. Occupied by the Philistines, their tribal allotment was too hard to take. So they head north to find another place to live. However, en route, they take Micah's priest, household idols and priestly garments, so that they can set up their own religious centre. The Danites persuade the priest: 'Isn't it better that you serve a tribe and clan in Israel as priest rather than just one man's household?' (Judges 18:19). We last see poor old Micah shouting at the Danites to bring back his idol and priest, but returning home empty-handed. What had begun as a home-brew religion goes on to become the public shrine of Dan, leading to their judgment and downfall later. Interestingly, Dan is a tribe that disappears from the later record and is absent from the list of tribes in the New Testament (Revelation 7:4–8). What began as a little domestic idolatry led to the destruction of an entire tribe.

The arms race

Technology and progress often go hand in hand with military

needs. The twentieth-century space race and development of rocket technology were clearly related to the military competition between the superpowers. Same thing in the ancient world.

When Israel first entered the land, the people formed what is called a militia. That meant that every adult male, over the age of twenty, was expected to serve in the army (Numbers 1:3). It would take the establishment of a central administration, under the kings, to develop a professional, standing army.

Armaments developed over the biblical period. In the book of Judges, we see a very loose collection of improvised weaponry, including ox-goads (Judges 3:31), animal jawbones (Judges 15:16) and slings (Judges 20:16). While these could make effective weapons, there is nothing quite like a sword (Judges 3:16) for success!

Swords, arrows and spears all benefitted from the ability of their makers to work metal, and in this, Israel were clearly out-classed by the Philistines (1 Samuel 13:19–22). Only Saul and Jonathan had metal weapons, so no doubt their army had to make do with improvising. The period of the judges and early monarchy lies just on the borderline between what we have called the Bronze

Left: Assyrian soldiers with slings march against a city near Jerusalem. Right: the sling was an effective weapon, especially in the hands of a professional soldier.

The Sumerians developed these heavy and unwieldy chariots.

Age and the Iron Age. The Israelites had been familiar with bronze during their time in Egypt, and many of the metal fittings for the tabernacle are described as bronze. But the Philistines were technologically superior and knew how to work iron. For all his heavy bronze armour, the Bible draws attention to the sharper, lighter iron point of Goliath's spear (1 Samuel 17:7).

One of the most effective pieces of military hardware in the ancient world was the chariot. The earliest chariots were cumbersome and probably had little value. Sumerian chariots were heavy, armoured wheeled wagons. Images portray them as slow, with poor manoeuvrability. But the later Hittite and Egyptian Empires recognized that the principle was good, and developed their technology further. The Egyptians developed lightweight chariots, with a very tight turning circle. They needed only two occupants: a driver and an archer. A unit of several chariots working together could deliver a barrage of deadly arrows, in a way that would foreshadow the development of the automatic machine-gun in the modern world.

Egypt's war chariots were probably the best in the ancient world (Exodus 14:5–7), but their pursuit of the Israelites over the Sea of Reeds revealed their limitations (Exodus 14:25). A chariot only works well on flat, open, dry terrain, perfect for pitched battles on a valley floor. The exposed seabed was not good for poor Pharaoh's chariots. This also explains why the

The war chariot of Rameses II—lighter, faster and more mpg than the earlier Sumerian models!

Philistines were able to keep the Israelite foot soldiers at bay with their chariot force. Commanding the coastal strip, here their chariots were the perfect weapon of war.

Without chariots, the early Israelites had to rely on guerrilla tactics. We see this, for example, in a skirmish during the time when Deborah was judge.

Sisera, commander of a Canaanite army, had 900 chariots 'fitted with iron' at his disposal (Judges 4:3), a formidable force by any ancient standards. Deborah takes on Sisera with her Israelite foot soldiers and a clever strategy. She has her commander, Barak, hide a large force on Mount Tabor. Meanwhile, Deborah uses a detachment to lead Sisera's chariot army along the River Kishon towards Mount Tabor. Knowledge of the topography reveals what is going on here.

The River Kishon leads the chariots further from the open plains into marshy ground near Mount Tabor. They are lured into a territory where the Israelite foot soldiers have the advantage. A rainstorm turns the terrain to mud (Judges 5:4). The chariots are stuck and not manoeuvrable. Even General Sisera has to abandon his and flee on foot (Judges 4:15). There is a rout, and the Canaanites are defeated. Any advantage of a chariot is lost in these conditions.

However, the Israelites were aware that chariots had great

value in battle. King David had one (1 Samuel 8:11), and Solomon built an extensive chariot army. The numbers of Solomon's force are unclear, but suggest that he had 1,400 chariots.[8] This would have been a large and formidable force, though not of great use in the central hill country. The last sight in the Old Testament of Israel's chariots reveals that, under King Jehoahaz, they numbered a grand total of ten (2 Kings 13:7). The writing was now on the wall for Israel.

City under siege

As we have seen in the story of Deborah's success, the key to victory is being able to choose your terrain. Many battles were fought in the open. But probably the best strategy for a people under attack was to build strong defences and play a waiting game.

Cities could be under siege for months. With the rural population gathered inside the walls, and the gates secure, it became a question of whose supplies would run out first. The attackers would soon consume the local resources and, as time went by, might give up and go home. The defenders had to rely on massive grain stores and a protected water source for survival.

King Hezekiah made provision for an oncoming siege by ensuring that the spring just outside Jerusalem's city wall was hidden and diverted through a tunnel, cut through rock to bring water into the city (2 Kings 20:20). This is still visible today, and most tourists will take the time to splash through the 1,750-foot-long underground water course in total darkness, awed by this remarkable feat of engineering. But the principle was common to ancient cities, and similar, though shorter, tunnels can be seen at Hazor (82 ft) and Megiddo (262 ft).

Cities were built to withstand sieges by being situated on high ground. The slopes at the base of the walls were deliberately built up and plastered, in what is called a 'glacis'. This would have been difficult to climb, and made it harder for those attacking to dig under the walls and undermine the foundations. The walls themselves could be solid or, better still, casemate. This was a system of two parallel walls, the outer thicker than the inner. Between the walls there was room for storage, or the space could even be incorporated into a domestic dwelling. The roof space between the two walls provided a commanding position for city defenders. We know that King Hezekiah built new walls for Jerusalem, to protect his people from the oncoming Assyrians, in 701 BC. The excavations of these walls reveal an impressive construction. His broad wall is 23 ft thick and would have risen 27 ft high.

The weakest point of the wall was the gateway. Gates developed into a system of doorways. We have already seen how King Solomon was instrumental in developing a new and effective gate architecture that became common in Israel. The roadway leading up to the city entrance would have had to take a left turn before entering the gate. This would always expose the attacking soldier's right side, unprotected by a shield and vulnerable to arrows. The six-chambered gate complex required the attackers to destroy a set of three major gates, each defended by a unit of soldiers. All the time they were pressing this attack, they were at the mercy of missile fire from above. This explains why the Bible describes the city gate as the location of the 'fiercest' fighting (2 Samuel 11:15).

King David knew an anecdotal story of a general killed by falling debris: 'Who killed Abimelek son of Jerub-Besheth? Didn't a woman drop an upper millstone on him from the wall, so that he died in Thebez? Why did you get so close to the wall?' (2 Samuel 11:21). Abimelek was leading an attack on a city gate when he came under this enemy fire and a well-timed millstone (Judges 9:50–53).

Life under siege must have been unbearable. The population

would have been much greater than normal, and sanitation terrible (2 Kings 18:27). With a lack of available food, inhabitants might even turn to cannibalism (Jeremiah 19:9). However, the attackers did not always have the time or resources to slowly starve the inhabitants. The great empires of the ancient world developed formidable siege engines to hasten victory. Wall reliefs from Assyria reveal the kind of technological weapons they brought into Canaan when they destroyed the northern kingdom. Heading down into Judah, they besieged the city of Lachish, not far from Jerusalem (2 Kings 18:13–14).

The siege and fall of Lachish are recorded in stunning detail by a wall relief, now housed at the British Museum in London.[9] The weapons of the Assyrian army are clearly depicted. Wooden roadways are laid up against the glacis to allow access to the city walls. Enormous siege engines, like ancient tanks, are hauled up the roadways to deliver blows against the walls themselves. From the siege engines, a variety of projectiles are launched against the inhabitants. And from their towers, the Israelites fight back. Burning missiles are fired against the siege engines to attempt to set them on fire. But the Assyrians have equipped their vehicles with water-based fire extinguishers. Down below them, ladders

Assyrian siege engine, with armour, battering ram and tower for archers.

are thrown up against the walls and, by force of numbers, the Assyrians are able to press the attack inside the city.

Eventually, the city falls to King Sennacherib, and final scenes show the Israelites taken captive and the city of Lachish providing a base camp for the king's intentions to take the battle on to Jerusalem. While he will succeed in laying siege to Jerusalem, he fails in his task and returns home defeated. His palace walls would preserve a record of the fall of Lachish, but his real objective had failed. So there should have been a wall relief of the fall of Jerusalem, but God protected that city.

Bible field trip

Reading: 2 Chronicles 36:15–23
Date: 539 BC
Destination: Jerusalem

1. How did the people respond to God's words (verses 15–16)?

2. How did the Babylonians deal with the people and possessions of Jerusalem when they invaded in 586 BC (verses 17–20)?

3. What does this passage tell us about God's purposes (verses 15, 16, 17, 21, 22)?

4. What is the real reason for the decree of King Cyrus of Persia (verses 22–23)?

9

BACK TO THE FUTURE

We have glimpsed our ancient ancestors and events across the Fertile Crescent, centuries before Julius Caesar first trod on England's soil. But what about the future? Can the Bible direct us into the distant future and show us what is still to come?

The Israelites gradually learned more of God and the purpose of life, as time went by. With the benefit of the complete Scriptures before us, we are at a distinct advantage. We certainly know more about the destination of this story than the average ancient Israelite could have done. Theologians sometimes use the term 'progressive revelation' to describe the way God unfolds knowledge over time. The ancient Israelites gradually came to understand our future destination, and what they thought of the future is what we will consider now. But most pressingly, what did they think about death?

What happens when we die?

Ancient religions shared our preoccupation with death. Stone

Age burials reveal bodies laid to rest, with adornments that suggest a widespread view of some kind of continued existence beyond the grave. Egyptian religion particularly is remembered for its preoccupation with death.

Mummified remains and lavish burials survived relatively well in the dry deserts of Egypt. Therefore, much of what remains of Ancient Egypt, seen today or on display in museums, reflects this particular concern with death. Among the remains are collections of spells known as the Book of the Dead. These were to help guide the deceased on their journey to the afterlife. This afterlife was open to everyone, but to get there, you had to travel on a boat. This required that you were light enough to make the journey. Your weight was not determined by a high-calorie diet, but by your deeds. Enough good deeds and you would be light enough to make the journey; too many bad ones and you would not. The Egyptian Book of the Dead also maintains a permanent connection between our soul in the afterlife and our physical remains in this present life. That is why the body had to be preserved and carefully laid to rest. If it were destroyed or went missing, then your soul would be lost too. Grave robbing was a serious crime in ancient Egypt.

The extravagant tombs of the pharaohs were obviously far beyond the reach of ordinary Egyptians, but everyone shared this concern with protecting their soul in the afterlife. Simpler burials in the desert, wrapped in cloth and accompanied by a few choice items, would also have ensured the preservation of the body for many years. Those who had pet cats and dogs could have them mummified too, so that they could continue to enjoy their company in the life to come.

Of course, the famous words of film director Woody Allen have probably always rung true: 'I don't want to achieve immortality through my work. I want to achieve immortality through not dying.' So is it possible to escape death?

Dodging death

One of the earliest stories ever found is the haunting and beautiful Epic of Gilgamesh, whom we met earlier. Many copies of this story, originally composed by the Sumerians long before Abraham, have been found in ancient archives. The epic is of great interest to biblical scholars, because it contains an account of the flood not unlike that in Genesis. But the main theme of the story is a friendship between King Gilgamesh of Uruk and his friend Enkidu.[1]

When Enkidu is sentenced to death by the gods, Gilgamesh embarks on a quest to find the secret of eternal life. This leads him to the man who built an ark during the great flood and received immortality: Utnapishtim. This 'Babylonian Noah' gives Gilgamesh little hope, pointing out that his own immortality was given as a gift. However, he does tell him that, deep beneath the waters, there is still a plant growing that can restore his youth. Gilgamesh explores the ocean bottom and retrieves some of this plant of eternal youth. Could this be some last remains of the tree of life from the garden in Eden, now submerged beneath floodwaters? Sadly, Gilgamesh never gets to try out their effectiveness. On his journey home, a crafty serpent steals the plant, and all hope of cheating death is gone.[2]

Genesis describes eternal life as a gift. Death was not God's original intention for Adam and Eve. By eating from the tree of life, they were to live forever. In their disobedience, they were cut off from the tree of life and then faced death. Perhaps Utnapishtim's words to Gilgamesh carry a theological truth. Eternal life is not to be found by cheating death, but by receiving a gift. The Israelites were aware of this in their worship. Liberation from slavery came as a gift. Torah was a gift. The land itself was given to them as an act of God's undeserved mercy. Could God even give a gift that would transcend death itself?

Let the dead bury the dead

The common view among theologians is that the ancient Israelites had little interest in life beyond the grave. During the period of the monarchy, their main concern was to have children and hope that the nation would prosper for generations to come. Death was a vague, shadowy destination, where a common fate awaited all. The more sophisticated themes of heaven and hell, along with the idea of a bodily resurrection, are thought to have emerged only late in Israel's history, some time after the exile of Judah in Babylon.[3]

The truth in this common scholarly view is that the Israelite understanding of the afterlife emerged only gradually over time. However, it is a misleading picture. There are glimmers of optimism and hope, even in the earliest books of the Old Testament. While the Israelites may not always have had a fully developed view of the life to come, they did have a healthy suspicion that God had purposes that even death could not disrupt.

A bodily burial was always important for the Israelites, and cremation was practically unknown.[4] Abraham bought a cave in which to bury his wife, Sarah, and this seems to belong to a common pattern of burial practice among the Israelites. Jacob and Joseph were both embalmed in the Egyptian way, but that was because they died in Egypt. Otherwise, bodies were laid to rest in the ground or in a rock-cut cavern.

The cave burial involved laying out a body on a stone bench, where it was allowed to decompose over about a year. Then relatives could collect the bones and place them in a recess in the wall, where earlier bones remained. It is this practice of gathering the bones together that lies behind the biblical expression: 'gathered to his people' (Genesis 49:33). The cave was sealed with a stone, but could be opened when necessary for new burials or the gathering of bones. The smell would have been terrible, and so, with the exception of kings, these burials always took place outside the city walls.

In 2002, a stone box made the news because it carried the Aramaic inscription: 'James son of Joseph brother of Jesus'. Dating to the time of Jesus, it was the kind of box used for collecting the bones of a corpse after the period of decomposition. These bone boxes are called 'ossuaries', and many have been found from the first century. Whether this particular one belonged to the James we know from the Bible is a matter of great debate. The use of ossuaries in burials belongs to only a brief period of Israel's history (c.20 BC–70 AD). But this use of bone boxes reflects the development in the time of Jesus of simpler burial customs, dating far back in Israel's earlier history.[5]

The rock-cut tomb was probably the preserve of the wealthy; for many people a grave was more likely dug in the ground. Any traces of their presence have long gone. But the practice of the cave burial does shed light on what the Israelites believed about the afterlife. It is not unreasonable to assume they held some kind of optimistic view of the future from the way they cared for physical remains.

Grave words

The Hebrew word *sheol* appears sixty-five times in the Old Testament, and is thought to mean something like 'grave' or 'netherworld'. With little evidence of its use outside the Bible, it is difficult to be certain about its meaning.

The grave (*sheol*) is the common fate of both the righteous and the wicked, a pit in the depths of the earth (Isaiah 14:15), dark and shadowy. But is this the whole story? Enoch (Genesis 5:24) and Elijah (2 Kings 2:11) avoid the grave altogether and are taken directly to God's presence. This at least indicates the possibility of a future destination other than the grave.

The law ruled out the practice of necromancy or contacting the dead. But although it was against God's law, the Israelites were clearly convinced that it could be done. It was a common practice of the Canaanite peoples, and King Saul indulged in it when he wanted advice from his dead counsellor, Samuel. In keeping with God's law, Saul had expelled all the mediums and spiritists (1 Samuel 28:3), but now, in need, he goes in search of one himself. These were people who traded in contacting the dead on behalf of relatives. Saul meets a woman who works some kind of necromancy and says, 'I see a ghostly figure coming up out of the earth' (1 Samuel 28:13). We know from sources outside the Bible that this kind of necromancy involved digging a pit in the earth and saying spells over it at night. The incident described here seems to follow that same pattern, with Saul arriving at night and a ghostly resemblance of Samuel arising out of the earth. We do not know the exact nature of Saul's vision, but the incident does demonstrate the Israelite conviction that death was not the end.

The book of Genesis describes death as a judgment on sin, rather than simply a natural process. This explains why a dead body is counted as unclean in the law (Numbers 19:16): death and sin are closely associated. The grave is a place of judgment. But this very fact offers consolation. If death were nothing more than the termination of life, then it would offer no possibility for wrongs being put right. But the ancient Israelites did have the hope that death would not have the last word. In his suffering, Job speaks these words of faith:

> I know that my redeemer lives,
>> and that in the end he will stand on the earth.
>
> And after my skin has been destroyed,
>> yet in my flesh I will see God;
>
> I myself will see him
>> with my own eyes—I, and not another.
>>
>> How my heart yearns within me!
>
> (Job 19:25–27)

These are not the words of a man who believes that death is the end. In his emotional and physical suffering, Job maintains a trust not only in a life to come, but in a personal encounter with God. Reference to a Redeemer is striking here. The grave is described as a prison, and freedom from a prison requires a payment.

In a psalm, the author recognizes the problem of redemption from death:

> No one can redeem the life of another
>> or give to God a ransom for them –
>
> the ransom for a life is costly,
>> no payment is ever enough –
>
> so that they should live on for ever
>> and not see decay.
>
> (Psalm 49:7–9)

Death does seem hopeless, because the price of redemption is too high. However, the psalmist then introduces a distinction between those who trust in wealth: 'Their forms will decay in the grave' (verse 14) and those whom God will 'redeem' (verse 15). Though no human being can pay the price for redemption, it seems that it is possible for God to do so.[6]

Though the grave is a gloomy place, it does not have the last word. God is in control even here: 'If I make my bed in the depths [*sheol*], you are there' (Psalm 139:8). The ancient Israelites did not have a developed understanding of eternal life and all that lay ahead, but they did have reason for optimism, found in the power of God himself. In his study of the term *sheol*, Desmond Alexander concludes,

> Whereas the wicked were thought to remain in the dark, silent region of Sheol, the righteous lived in the hope that God would deliver them from the power of death and take them to himself.[7]

In the unfolding revelation of God, this hope would become clearer still as Old Testament history progressed.

The physical resurrection

The importance of treating the body with respect and preserving the bones reflected the Israelite awareness that the human being was always intended to be an embodied being. Among the Greek philosophers and the Eastern religions, there would be a more ethereal view of our identity: the body was a prison from which our soul could be liberated to enjoy a more spiritual state of existence. But such language is alien to the Hebrew worldview.

The bones were gathered and preserved, because the Israelites hoped for a resurrection of the body in a future state. Whatever *sheol* might be, it was only a temporary, intermediate state, before this resurrection to come.

The hope of the Israelites was in a day when God would

wake the dead. Isaiah describes this in terms of joy and new birth:

> But your dead will live, Lord;
>   their bodies will rise –
> let those who dwell in the dust
>   wake up and shout for joy –
> your dew is like the dew of the morning;
>   the earth will give birth to her dead.
> (Isaiah 26:19)

Like a new day, there will be a return to life for the dead. Waking up with a shout of joy, the night of sleep in the grave will be over. Isaiah speaks of 'your dead' as if some of the dead belong to the Lord. But what of those who do not? The book of Daniel, perhaps one of the last books of the Old Testament, presents the clearest statement of the resurrection: 'Multitudes who sleep in the dust of the earth will awake: some to everlasting life, others to shame and everlasting contempt' (Daniel 12:2). This image of the soul being asleep in death seems to fit very well with the picture of the grave as a bed, but the New Testament continues to clarify the details. In some sense, there is an intermediate state when God's people live in his presence, while they await this final resurrection (Revelation 7:9).

This theme of bodily resurrection develops through the Old Testament, but the seeds of this idea are found in the earliest writings. Not even the grave can separate the Lord's people from their God. He has jurisdiction over death and life. How will the redemption price be paid? The clue was already provided in the sacrificial system. As Israelites offered up their pigeons, lambs and goats, they recognized the principle of substitution.

A life could be offered in place of a life, to redeem someone from the judgment they deserve. However, no fellow human could offer such a perfect sacrifice. Nor could pigeons or lambs. These were all like signposts in the ancient world, pointing to a perfect Redeemer. Jesus Christ, who knew no sin, became sin for us, so that we might become the righteousness of God. Now that the price has been paid, we are redeemed from sin's punishment. Consequently, death can no longer be our prison. Quoting words from the prophet Hosea, Paul asks,

'Where, O death, is your victory?
    Where, O death, is your sting?'

The sting of death is sin, and the power of sin is the law. But thanks be to God! He gives us the victory through our Lord Jesus Christ.
(1 Corinthians 15:55–57)

This is the Redeemer that Job spoke of many centuries earlier, and one day Paul and Job will both rise from the dead in their new resurrection bodies.

Prophet and loss

God provided priests and prophets to offer spiritual guidance to the people. The priests were drawn from the tribe of Levi and were to serve in the tabernacle and temple. As we have seen, there were renegade priests like those of the Danites, who assisted the people in setting up alternative shrines for worship. The prophets had a different function. They spoke the words of God to the people.

Who exactly were the prophets? Unlike priests, a prophet

was not appointed as a professional by birth, but was specially equipped by God, through the Spirit, for the task.

Prophecy is an ambiguous word. It is often taken to mean 'foretelling', and it is assumed that prophets predicted the future. But it is better to take the word to mean 'forth telling', because while a prophet 'tells forth' God's Word, he may not say anything about future events. Prophecy may well include prediction, but it need not. God tells Moses that, when he raises up a prophet, 'I will put my words in his mouth' (Deuteronomy 18:18). The prophet would be a mouthpiece for God. Of course, that would also lend itself to abuse, as someone might wrongly claim to be a prophet. A prophet must speak only what God has commanded, only in the name of the Lord, and if a prediction is made that does not come true, then that is evidence of a false prophet (Deuteronomy 18:20–22).

The first man identified as a prophet in the Bible is Abraham (Genesis 20:7). Though about fifty different people are called prophets in the Bible, many thousands more are referred to, but left unnamed. Sometimes a prophet is simply called a 'man of God' (1 Kings 13:1). Many wandered the land of Israel and depended on people's hospitality. Elijah benefitted from generous provision on his travels. A widow during a famine in the region of Sidon shared what little she had, so that she and he could eat (1 Kings 17:12).

A professional class of prophets seems to have arisen in the land. The first mention of such a gathering is in 1 Samuel 10:5, where we see them prophesying in a procession, accompanied by what sounds like a boisterous music band. A company of prophets was located at Jericho, and Elijah may have been a visiting teacher there (2 Kings 2:4–5). However, a professional class leaves itself open to abuse.

Amos describes his own call to be a prophet in eighth-century Israel:

> I was neither a prophet nor the son of a prophet, but I was a shepherd, and I also took care of sycamore-fig trees. But the LORD took me from tending the flock and said to me, 'Go, prophesy to my people Israel.'
> (Amos 7:14–15)

Amos was a professional farmer. With a farm in Tekoa, not far from Jerusalem in Judah, it would have been a bold move for him to leave his fields and head north to deliver God's Word in the rival kingdom of Israel.

God's prophetic Word was often a revelation of the real meaning of events. As empires rose and fell, and invaders came and went, the Israelites would have asked themselves whether or not these were just the chance events of world history. Through the prophets, God revealed that he had a purpose and plan unfolding in history. Nations could experience blessing or judgment. Sometimes the people of God were being punished; at other times they were being blessed.

Through the prophets, God reveals the promise that life would not always be this way. Death, destruction and war would not have the last word. This theme becomes increasingly significant as the Old Testament heads towards its fulfilment.

Covenant

The Jews call the books we have been considering 'The Hebrew Scriptures', while Christians call them 'The Old Testament'. Apart from a difference in order, they are the same books. The word *testament* is used to describe a legally binding written promise. It is a synonym for *covenant*. The existence of a New Testament or covenant shows that Christians believe the Old still forms part of the one Bible, but that Jesus brought about a new development in how we relate to God.

In many ways, the Old Testament is a disappointing book. It seems that, no matter how much God provides for and blesses his people, they prefer to turn away and do things their own way. Whether it is Adam and Eve, Abraham and Sarah, Moses and the Israelites, or David and Bathsheba, the stories we have read are, partly, stories of disobedience.

God made a covenant with Abram to create a great nation. As originally intended for Adam and Eve in creation, his people were to multiply in number and bring blessing to the earth. Ancient Israel glimpsed something of that blessing. They knew a land of milk and honey and a law that provided peace and security. But something remained wrong deep down in the human heart. Even King David, the man after God's own heart, fell far short of God's holy standards.

So the prophets foresaw a new covenant in which the human heart would be changed. This would involve forgiveness, cleansing and transformation:

> I will sprinkle clean water on you, and you will be clean; I will
> cleanse you from all your impurities and from all your idols.
> I will give you a new heart and put a new spirit in you. . . .
> I will put my Spirit in you and move you to follow my decrees
> and be careful to keep my laws.
> (Ezekiel 36:25–27)

This promise of the Holy Spirit, not unique to Ezekiel, marks a new stage in God's redemptive plan to renew creation. The Holy Spirit will regenerate the human heart to give us a new desire to do God's will.[8]

The prophet Jeremiah describes a new covenant with Israel, when God says,

I will put my law in their minds
and write it on their hearts.
I will be their God,
and they will be my people.
(Jeremiah 31:33)

This new covenant will not be accessed through perfect obedience. The Old Testament proves that this has never been possible, but God says,

I will forgive their wickedness
and will remember their sins no more.
(Jeremiah 31:34)

So the prophets foresee a new covenant, marked by the work of the Holy Spirit, bringing forgiveness and transformation. Through the prophet Joel, God reveals a time when 'I will pour out my Spirit on all people' (Joel 2:28). The apostle Peter would take up those words to help us understand what was happening on the day of Pentecost. When God poured out the Spirit on the first Christians in the book of Acts, Joel's words provided the interpretation. Jesus had brought about a new covenant, through his death and resurrection.

For an ancient Israelite, the promises of Scripture spoke of the faithfulness of a God with plans to bless and not harm his people. They had to live by faith in those promises.

Jesus Christ has now come. He is the fulfilment of the promises. He now sends out his followers not just to a region in the Middle East, but to the ends of the earth. What had been modelled for us of God's mercy and holiness in the Old Testament was expanded and opened up to the whole world. It had always been God's plan to have a vast number of people, blessing the whole earth (Genesis 1:28), and now, through Christ, that global mission has become a reality.

We are no longer ancient Israelites. While we can glimpse the world as they did, and that helps us to understand their Scriptures, we now read the Old Testament in the light of Christ. Returning to the present, we find that these books are not an alien world after all. They are not there simply to tell us about ancient history, unusual customs or even philosophical ideas about life after death. These great writings prepare us for Christ, and as we read them we find him:

> You study the Scriptures diligently because you think that in them you have eternal life. These are the very Scriptures that testify about me, yet you refuse to come to me to have life. (John 5:39)

Having travelled back to the world of ancient Israel, our attention is drawn to Jesus Christ. He is the real point of the story. He is the central point of history. I hope you have found our survey helpful, and that it opens up new avenues for you to time travel other corridors of ancient history. But I also hope that you find the real point of this story, in the significance of who Jesus really is. Not only a time lord, Jesus Christ is the Lord of time.

Bible field trip

Reading: Hebrews 11:1–12:2
Date: The future
Destination: New creation

1. What homeland were the ancient Israelites seeking (verses 13–16)?

2. How many different ways did these people show their faith in action?

3. How did many of these people deal with suffering and rejection?

4. What should we learn from the stories of these ancient people (12:1–2)?

FURTHER READING

Old Testament overview

Graeme Goldsworthy, *According to Plan: The Unfolding Revelation of God in the Bible* (Leicester: IVP, 1991).

Alec Motyer, *Discovering the Old Testament* (Leicester: Crossway, 2006).

John H. Walton and Andrew E. Hill, *Old Testament Today: A Journey from Original Meaning to Contemporary Significance* (Grand Rapids: Zondervan, 2004).

John H. Walton, Victor H. Matthews and Mark W. Chavalas, *The IVP Bible Background Commentary: Old Testament* (Leicester: IVP, 2000).

Philip Yancey, *The Bible Jesus Read* (Grand Rapids: Zondervan, 1999).

Archaeological background to the Old Testament

John D. Currid and David P. Barrett, *ESV Bible Atlas* (Wheaton, IL: Crossway, 2010).

Adrian Curtis, *Oxford Bible Atlas* (Oxford: Oxford University Press, 2007).

Brian Edwards and Clive Anderson, *Through the British Museum with the Bible*, 3rd ed. (Leominster: Day One, 2011).

James K. Hoffmeier, *The Archaeology of the Bible* (London: Lion, 2008).

Walter C. Kaiser, *The Old Testament Documents: Are They Reliable and Relevant?* (Leicester: IVP, 2001).

Walter C. Kaiser and Duane A. Garrett (eds.), *Archaeological Study Bible: An Illustrated Walk through Biblical History and Culture* (Grand Rapids: Zondervan, 2006).

K. A. Kitchen, *On the Reliability of the Old Testament* (Grand Rapids: Eerdmans, 2003).

Victor H. Matthews, *Studying the Ancient Israelites: A Guide to Sources and Methods* (Nottingham: Apollos, 2007).

Alan Millard, *Discoveries from Bible Times* (London: Lion, 1997).

Jerome Murphy-O'Connor, *Oxford Archaeological Guides: The Holy Land* (Oxford: Oxford University Press, 1998).

Randall Price, *The Stones Cry Out* (Eugene, OR: Harvest House, 1997).

Hershel Shanks (ed.), *Ancient Israel: From Abraham to the Roman Destruction of the Temple*, 3rd ed. (Washington, DC: Biblical Archaeology Society/Prentice Hall, 2011).

Storytelling and Hebrew narrative

Robert Alter, *The Art of Biblical Narrative* (New York: Basic, 1981).

Dale Ralph Davis, *The Word Became Fresh* (Ross-shire: Christian Focus, 2006).

V. Philips Long, *The Art of Biblical History* (Leicester: Apollos, 1994).

Tremper Longman III, *How to Read Genesis* (Downers Grove, IL: IVP, 2005).

Alan Millard, *Reading and Writing in the Time of Jesus* (Sheffield: Sheffield Academic Press, 2001).

Susan Niditch, *Oral World and Written Word: Ancient Israelite Literature* (Louisville, KY: Westminster John Knox, 1996).

Old Testament theology

C. John Collins, *Did Adam and Eve Really Exist? Who They Were and Why It Matters* (Nottingham: IVP, 2011).

David E. Holwerda, *Jesus and Israel: One Covenant or Two?* (Leicester: Apollos, 1995).

Philip S. Johnston, *Shades of Sheol: Death and Afterlife in the Old Testament* (Leicester: Apollos, 2002).

Hetty Lalleman, *Celebrating the Law* (Carlisle: Authentic Media, 2004).

Tremper Longman III, *Making Sense of the Old Testament: Three Crucial Questions* (Grand Rapids: Baker, 1998).

Sydney H. T. Page, *Powers of Evil: A Biblical Study of Satan and Demons* (Leicester: Apollos, 1995).

Vern Poythress, *Christian Interpretations of Genesis 1* (Phillipsburg, NJ: P&R, 2013).

Philip S. Ross, *From the Finger of God: The Biblical and Theological Basis for the Threefold Division of the Law* (Ross-shire: Christian Focus, 2010).

Robin Routledge, *Old Testament Theology: A Thematic Approach* (Nottingham: IVP, 2008).

John H. Walton, *Ancient Near Eastern Thought and the Old Testament* (Nottingham: Apollos, 2007).

John H. Walton, *The Lost World of Genesis One: Ancient Cosmology and the Origins Debate* (Downers Grove, IL: IVP, 2009).

Christopher J. H. Wright, *Old Testament Ethics for the People of God* (Leicester: IVP, 2004).

The Old Testament social world

Clive Anderson, *Sennacherib* (Leominster: Day One, 2007).

Bill T. Arnold and Bryan E. Beyer, *Readings from the Ancient Near East* (Grand Rapids: Zondervan, 2002).

Daniel I. Block, *The Gods of the Nations: Studies in Ancient Near Eastern National Theology* (Grand Rapids: Baker, 2000).

Paul Copan, *Is God a Moral Monster? Making Sense of the Old Testament God* (Grand Rapids: Baker, 2011).

John D. Currid, *The Ancient Near East and the Old Testament* (Grand Rapids: Baker, 1987).

William Dever, *The Lives of Ordinary People in Ancient Israel* (Cambridge: Eerdmans, 2012).

Volkmar Fritz, *The City in Ancient Israel* (Sheffield: Sheffield Academic Press, 1995).

Alfred J. Hoerth, Gerald L. Mattingly and Edwin M. Yamauchi (eds.), *Peoples of the Old Testament World* (Grand Rapids: Baker, 1994).

Philip J. King and Lawrence E. Stager, *Life in Biblical Israel* (Louisville, KY: Westminster John Knox, 2001).

Victor Matthews, *Manners and Customs in the Bible* (Peabody, MA: Hendrickson, 1988).

Jonathan N. Tubb, *The Canaanites* (London: British Museum Press, 1998).

NOTES

1. Preparing to embark

1. This writer is happy to use and recommend the New International Version 2011, from which all quotations are taken in this book. There is no perfect translation, but following the principle of dynamic equivalence, the NIV strikes a good balance between accuracy and readability.

2. Paul knows that Christ has now defeated the work of Satan, in fulfilment of the promise in Genesis: 'The God of peace will soon crush Satan under your feet' (Romans 16:20).

3. A comprehensive explanation of how particular Old Testament texts are used in the New is found in G. K. Beale and D. A. Carson (eds.), *Commentary on the New Testament Use of the Old Testament* (Nottingham: Apollos, 2008).

2. Hebrew storytelling

1. Sadly, between the time of the judges and the much later King Josiah (reigned c.640–609 BC), we read that the Passover was not celebrated by God's people as a nation (2 Kings 23:21–23). No doubt, families and good kings did celebrate, but as a national celebration it was allowed to lapse.

2. Robert Alter, *The Art of Biblical Narrative* (New York: Basic, 1981), p. 32.

3. V. Philips Long, *The Art of Biblical History* (Leicester: Apollos, 1994), p. 74.

4. One other Bible book has only a passing reference to God (Song of Songs 8:6).

5. Dale Ralph Davis, *The Word Became Fresh* (Ross-shire, Christian Focus, 2006), p. 22.

6. Ibid., p. 13.

7. To describe the oral traditions does not imply that the Bible began as oral stories that were later written down. That may be true in places but, as a general rule, is wide of the mark. The stories in the Bible have clear literary form, and it is just guesswork to claim that they first did the rounds as oral stories. For more on this, see Susan Niditch (1996; see note 8 below) and her critique of earlier scholarly ideas. However, the written words were intended for oral repetition, and so it is not surprising that these written accounts lend themselves to memorization and public reading. The development of this process into New Testament times is given a comprehensive survey in Alan Millard, *Reading and Writing in the Time of Jesus* (Sheffield: Sheffield University Press, 2000).

8. Susan Niditch, *Oral World and Written Word: Ancient Israelite Literature* (Louisville, KY: Westminster John Knox, 1996), p. 13.

9. To understand this chiasm in detail, see Gordon J. Wenham, *Word Biblical Commentary, vol. 1: Genesis 1–15* (Waco, TX: Word, 1987), pp. 155ff.

10. Ibid., p. 157.

3. On location

1. Adrian Curtis, *Oxford Bible Atlas* (Oxford: Oxford University Press, 2007), p. 24.

2. Steven Collins and Latayne C. Scott, *Discovering the City of Sodom*

(London: Howard Books, 2013). Collins's claim remains controversial, as it dates the destruction to 1650 BC, when Tall el-Hammam was destroyed in a catastrophic fire. This is late for the period of Abraham.

3. For a technical description of this find, see Avi Gopher et al., 'Middle Pleistocene Dental Remains from Qesem Cave (Israel)', *American Journal of Physical Anthropology* 144 (April 2011), pp. 575–592. Gopher's press release that these finds could 'rewrite the history of human evolution' caused a media stir! It is certainly a reminder that the further back in the archaeological record we go, the more ambiguous the evidence becomes.

4. Going back to our roots

1. For a fuller discussion, see Duane A. Garrett, *Rethinking Genesis: The Sources and Authorship of the First Book of the Pentateuch* (Ross-shire: Christian Focus, 2000), pp. 87–103.

2. Colin Brown (ed.), *New International Dictionary of New Testament Theology*, vol. 2 (Carlisle: Paternoster, 1986), p. 643.

3. C. S. Lewis, 'Myth Became Fact', in Lesley Walmsley (ed.), *C. S. Lewis: Essay Collection and Other Short Pieces* (London: HarperCollins, 2000), p. 141.

4. Many readers will want a simple answer to an apparently simple question. How old is creation? The reality is that theologians recognise that there are complex issues in interpreting Genesis. For a very helpful guide through the options, see Vern Poythress, *Christian Interpretations of Genesis 1* (Phillipsburg, NJ: P&R, 2013).

5. Augustine, 'On the Literal Meaning of Genesis', Book I, 19, 39, in John E. Rotelle (ed.), *On Genesis* (New York: New City Press, 2002), p. 186.

6. Francis Schaeffer, *Genesis in Space and Time*, from *The Complete Works*, vol. 2 (Wheaton: Crossway, 1982).

7. Some Christians hold that creation has an appearance of great age, because processes that are very slow today were very fast at times in the ancient past. Peter reminds us that the way things happen today is not the way they have always been (2 Peter 3:4–6). See Douglas Kelly, *Creation and Change* (Ross-shire: Mentor, 1997). The debate among Christians will not be solved in this single chapter, but contrary views can be compared using well-presented cases from either side of the debate, such as Melvin Tinker, *Reclaiming Genesis* (London: Monarch, 2010), who holds that the earth is billions of years old, and Paul Garner, *The New Creationism* (Darlington: Evangelical Press, 2009), who maintains that the earth is very young, bearing only an appearance of old age. A helpful middle position, with which this author is in sympathy, is found in John Lennox, *Seven Days That Divide the World* (Grand Rapids: Zondervan, 2011). Lennox seeks to read Genesis as history in the light of contemporary science.

8. John H. Walton, *The NIV Application Commentary: Genesis* (Grand Rapids: Zondervan, 2001), p. 126.

9. A theme we cannot hope to pursue here, but given breathtaking explanation in G. K. Beale, *The Temple and the Church's Mission: A Biblical Theology of the Dwelling Place of God* (Leicester: Apollos, 2004).

10. A classic example of this is found in Henri Blocher, *In the Beginning: The Opening Chapters of Genesis* (Leicester: IVP, 1984).

11. Schaeffer, *Genesis in Space and Time*, p. 7.

12. C. John Collins, *Did Adam and Eve Really Exist?* (Nottingham: IVP, 2011), p. 134.

13. C. S. Lewis, *Prince Caspian* (London: Collins, 1997), p. 185.

14. The reference to 'people' in Job 31:33 uses the Hebrew *Adam* and can be understood as reference to his hiding in the garden. For more on this, see Collins, *Did Adam and Eve Really Exist?*

15. Blocher, *In the Beginning*, p. 170.
16. This kind of editorial updating to preserve our understanding happens elsewhere in Scripture. Genesis 14:14 refers to the city of Dan, though this city was known as Laish at that time. When the Israelite tribe of Dan settled the region, they gave the city their own name, long after the events of Genesis.
17. Tremper Longman III, *How to Read Genesis* (Downers Grove, IL: IVP), p. 127.
18. Schaeffer, *Genesis in Space and Time*, p. 35.

5. Meet the natives

 1. Bill T. Arnold and Bryan E. Beyer (eds.), *Readings from the Ancient Near East* (Grand Rapids: Baker, 2002), p. 71. The translation of Sumerian remains very uncertain, and there are variant readings. The world needs more scholars able to read and translate this ancient language. Could it be something you might be called to do?
 2. Perhaps this is alluded to in Joshua 24:2.
 3. Steven Collins, *Let My People Go! Using Historical Synchronisms to Identify the Pharaoh of the Exodus* (Albuquerque, NM: Trinity Southwest University Press, 2012). These synchronisms point to Tuthmosis IV as the pharaoh of the exodus.
 4. For the plausible account of the discovery of one such lost city and an example of what these early cities were like, see Steven Collins and Latayne C. Scott, *Discovering the City of Sodom* (London: Howard Books, 2013).
 5. Alan Millard, 'Amorites and Israelites: Invisible Invaders', in James K. Hoffmeier and Alan Millard (eds.), *The Future of Biblical Archaeology* (Grand Rapids: Eerdmans, 2004), p. 159.
 6. 'Far' is a relative term, a journey of 40 miles—not much in a car on a highway, but much more difficult in the ancient world!
 7. See D. A. Carson, 'Getting Excited about Melchizedek (Psalm 110)', in D. A. Carson (ed.), *The Scriptures Testify about Me* (Nottingham: IVP, 2013).

8. Ezekiel describes Jerusalem's father as an Amorite and his mother as a Hittite (Ezekiel 16:3). This is probably not a literal description of the city, but a picture of the spiritual condition of the Israelites.

9. This is called 'Caphtor', in Amos 9:7, and so they are also called the 'Caphtorites' elsewhere in the Bible (Deuteronomy 2:23).

6. Among many gods

1. G. J. Wenham, 'The Religion of the Patriarchs', in A. R. Millard and D. J. Wiseman (eds.), *Essays on the Patriarchal Narratives* (Leicester: IVP, 1980).

2. Daniel I. Block, *The New American Commentary: Judges–Ruth* (Nashville: Broadman & Holman, 1999). For a more sympathetic treatment of Jephthah and his misunderstanding, see Dale Ralph Davis, *Judges: Such a Great Salvation* (Ross-shire: Christian Focus, 2000), pp. 140–143.

3. Daniel Strange, in Gavin D'Costa, Paul F. Knitter and Daniel Strange, *Only One Way?* (London: SCM, 2011), p. 218.

4. A detailed description and clear identification of the unique divine status of Molech is found in John Day, *Molech: A God of Human Sacrifice in the Old Testament*, University of Cambridge Oriental Publications 41 (Cambridge: Cambridge University Press, 1989).

5. Plutarch, *On Superstition, 13*, in F. C. Babbitt (ed. and trans.), *Plutarch's Moralia*, vol. 2 (London: Loeb Classical Library, 1928), cited in Day, *Molech: A God of Human Sacrifice in the Old Testament*, p. 89.

6. The female goddess Ishtar was worshipped among the Sumerians. She was a goddess of sex, fertility and war. Associated with the planet Venus, she was known by the name Asherah in Canaan. Worship of this female fertility goddess involved prostitution (Exodus 34:13–16; 2 Kings 23:7).

7. An authoritative critique is offered by Shmuel Ahituv, 'Did God Really Have a Wife?' *Biblical Archaeology Review* 32:5 (Sept/Oct 2006), pp. 62–66.

8. John Day, *Yahweh and the Gods and Goddesses of Canaan* (Sheffield: Sheffield Academic Press, 2002), p. 233.

9. John N. Oswalt, *The Bible among the Myths: Unique Revelation or Just Ancient Literature?* (Grand Rapids: Zondervan, 2009), p. 107.

10. Alan Millard, *Discoveries from Bible Times* (London: Lion, 1997), p. 73.

11. K. A. Kitchen, *On the Reliability of the Old Testament* (Grand Rapids: Eerdmans, 2003), pp. 275–282.

12. Perhaps the most detailed contemporary work is found in Leen Ritmeyer, *The Quest: Revealing the Temple Mount in Jerusalem* (Jerusalem: Carta, 2006).

13. Where is the ark of the covenant today? To find an answer, you might watch the Hollywood blockbuster, *Raiders of the Lost Ark*, and wonder if it now lies in a United States storage facility. However, for a briefing on the facts about the ark, you can find an accurate overview in Nick Page, *What Happened to the Ark of the Covenant?* (Milton Keynes: Authentic Media, 2007), pp. 99–112. A popular tradition holds that it found its way to Ethiopia, where it remains closely guarded. A more likely suggestion is that later invaders melted down the gold and destroyed what was left. Sadly, the most likely scenario would make the least interesting movie script!

14. The NIV translates the Greek word for 'tabernacle' as 'dwelling', but the connection would not have been lost to the original readers of the Gospel.

15. N. T. Wright, *The Resurrection of the Son of God* (London: SPCK, 2003), pp. 671–672.

16. 1 Corinthians 3:16; 1 Timothy 3:15; Hebrews 12:22–23; 1 Peter 2:5.

7. Laying down the law

1. Cited in Jonathan F. Bayes, 'The Threefold Division of the Law'

(Newcastle: Christian Institute, 2005), a very helpful overview and defence of this position. A particularly robust presentation of this position is found in Philip S. Ross, *From the Finger of God: The Biblical and Theological Basis for the Threefold Division of the Law* (Ross-shire: Christian Focus, 2010). An alternative view is offered by Hetty Lalleman, *Celebrating the Law? Rethinking Old Testament Ethics* (Carlisle: Authentic Media, 2004) and Christopher J. H. Wright, *Old Testament Ethics for the People of God* (Leicester: IVP, 2004).

2. Alec Motyer, *Look to the Rock* (Leicester: IVP, 1996), p. 39.
3. Wright, *Old Testament Ethics for the People of God*, p. 38.
4. Ibid., p. 74.
5. A bacon double cheeseburger has the additional problem of being in breach of modern kosher food laws, which state that meat and dairy products should not be served together. These kosher laws are derived from the prohibition on cooking a baby goat in its mother's milk (Exodus 23:19).
6. Lalleman, *Celebrating the Law?* pp. 76–77.
7. Gordon J. Wenham, 'The Old Testament Attitude to Homosexuality', *Expository Times* 102 (1991), pp. 259–363.
8. For a closer discussion of the ethics of many difficult areas in the Old Testament law, see Paul Copan, *Is God a Moral Monster?* (Grand Rapids: Baker, 2011).

8. War and peace

1. See K. A. Kitchen, *On the Reliability of the Old Testament* (Grand Rapids: Eerdmans, 2003), pp. 261ff. The Hebrew *suph* means 'reed' or 'bulrushes', not 'red'. Hence, baby Moses was placed in a reed (*suph*) basket, not a red basket! (Exodus 2:3).
2. A detailed discussion of the archaeological issues surrounding the exodus is provided by James K. Hoffmeier, *Israel in Egypt* (Oxford: Oxford University Press, 1996).
3. David M. Fouts, 'The Demographics of Ancient Israel', *Biblical*

Research Bulletin 7:2 (Albuquerque, NM: Trinity Southwest University, 2007).

4. The same Hebrew word means something like a 'clan' in Judges 6:15. See J. W. Wenham, 'Large Numbers in the Old Testament', *Tyndale Bulletin* 18 (1967), pp. 10–16.

5. A mistake, based on a single period of earlier Egyptian history.

6. Kitchen, *On the Reliability of the Old Testament*, pp. 110–112.

7. The full story is found in Judges 17–18.

8. The references to his chariots and chariot horses confuse what the total may have been (1 Kings 4:26; 1 Kings 10:26; 2 Chronicles 9:25).

9. For a description of the battle and historical background to the Assyrian period, see Clive Anderson, *Sennacherib* (Leominster: Day One, 2007), pp. 16–25.

9. Back to the future

1. Uruk is another very early city. It is referred to in Scripture (Genesis 10:10, sometimes as 'Erech'), and its memory probably survives in the name of the modern region, Iraq. Gilgamesh is often associated with Nimrod, the mighty hunter in Genesis 10:8–9.

2. The story is easily available in modern translations. See Andrew George (trans.), *The Epic of Gilgamesh* (London: Penguin), 2003.

3. T. Desmond Alexander, 'The Old Testament View of Life after Death', *Themelios* 11:2 (1986), pp. 41–46.

4. Exceptions prove the rule (1 Samuel 31:12). Into modern times, most Jews avoid the practice, for theological reasons related to the Old Testament.

5. For a full description, see Jodi Magness, *Stone and Dung, Oil and Spit: Jewish Daily Life in the Time of Jesus* (Grand Rapids: Eerdmans, 2011), ch. 11.

6. The fate of those who are not redeemed is even more graphically described in Psalm 73.

7. Alexander, 'The Old Testament View of Life after Death', p. 45.
8. This is not to suggest that the Holy Spirit was absent in the Old Testament, far from it—see Christopher J. H. Wright, *Knowing the Holy Spirit through the Old Testament* (Oxford: Monarch, 2006).

SCRIPTURE INDEX

Old Testament

Genesis, 18, 21, 23, 24, 25, 31, 35, 40, 41, 46, 48, 49, 58, 61, 62, 63, 64, 69–70, 75, 77, 78, 79, 80, 82, 83, 84, 85, 90, 91, 92, 98, 102, 105, 110, 111, 118, 139, 140, 141, 164, 177, 178, 183, 187, 197n16, 201n1

Exodus, 34, 43, 57, 97–98, 102, 110, 143, 146, 149, 152, 153, 155, 159, 167, 198n6, 200n5

Leviticus, 18, 118, 135, 137, 138, 140, 141, 142, 145

Numbers, 19, 43, 45, 57, 58, 59, 142, 159, 166, 178

Deuteronomy, 19, 59, 62, 64, 75, 124, 137, 140, 142, 147, 160, 164, 183, 198n9

Joshua, 55, 61, 156–57, 160, 197n2

Judges, 40, 47, 50, 65, 66, 111, 164, 165, 166, 168, 170, 201n4, 201n7

Ruth, 140

1 Samuel, 35, 40, 64, 66, 68, 102, 108, 140, 160, 164, 166, 167, 168, 178, 183, 201n4

2 Samuel, 35, 43, 45, 159, 161, 170

1 Kings, 40, 44, 59, 67, 96, 97, 116, 117, 119, 120, 144, 155, 162, 164, 183, 201n8

2 Kings, 27, 76, 96, 104, 117, 121, 144, 164, 169, 171, 178, 183, 193n1, 198n6

1 Chronicles, 117, 122

2 Chronicles, 119, 120, 143, 172, 201n8

Ezra, 27, 107, 130

Esther, 38, 107

Job, 81, 122, 179, 196n14

Psalms, 44, 66, 75, 113, 134, 179, 180, 201n6

Proverbs, 66, 67

Ecclesiastes, 67

Song of Songs, 21, 194n4

Isaiah, 122, 129, 130, 178, 181

Jeremiah, 96, 113, 117, 171, 186

Ezekiel, 123, 144, 185, 198n8

Daniel, 27, 35, 106, 181

Hosea, 81, 133, 182

Joel, 186

Amos, 65, 184, 198n9

Jonah, 105
Micah, 135
Nahum, 67
Zechariah, 64

New Testament
Matthew, 20, 121, 128, 133, 143, 148, 149
Mark, 136, 140, 143
Luke, 22, 59–60, 70, 122, 129
John, 128, 187
Acts, 20, 22, 82, 136–37, 155, 186

Romans, 81, 84, 113, 141, 193n2
1 Corinthians, 20, 81, 182, 199n16
2 Corinthians, 138–39
Galatians, 84, 138
2 Thessalonians, 20
1 Timothy, 71, 137, 199n16
Hebrews, 30, 41, 85, 133, 164, 187, 199n16
1 Peter, 199n16
2 Peter, 17, 71, 196n7
Revelation, 20, 27, 31, 79, 165, 181

GENERAL INDEX

Abimelek, 46
Abraham, Abram, 18, 21, 25,
    35–36, 40–41, 42, 46, 62, 70, 79,
    82–85, 90, 92, 95, 98, 101, 102,
    110–11, 118, 139, 140, 176, 183,
    185
Adam, 23, 70, 77–82, 84, 87, 112,
    175, 185, 196n14
Ahaz, 104, 119
Akhenaten, 114–16
Ammon (Ammonites), 111–12,
    117
Amos, 183–84
animals, 20, 24, 43, 45, 56, 65–67,
    68, 93, 114, 118–19, 136–38,
    143–44, 164
ark of the covenant, 43, 125, 128,
    199n13
Asherah, 120–21, 198n6
Assyria (Assyrians), 26, 27, 55,
    96, 103–5, 141, 166, 170–72,
    201n9

Baal, 44, 116–23
Babel, Tower of, 82, 90

Babylon, 26, 27, 42, 55, 57, 58, 96,
    102, 105–7, 122–23, 130, 141,
    145–46, 172
Balaam, 45
Bathsheba, 44–45
Beersheba, 59, 62

Canaan (Canaanites), 16, 20, 25,
    26, 55–58, 61, 63, 65–66, 83, 85,
    98–102, 116–18, 142, 156–58,
    168
Carmel, Mount, 44, 119–20
Chemosh, 111–12
chiasm, 48–50
child sacrifice, 117–19
city, 58, 62, 68, 88, 99–101, 105,
    116, 157–58, 160–63, 169–72
covenant, 49, 128, 184–87
creation, 21, 23, 31, 46, 70, 72–73,
    74–78, 114, 139, 140–41, 195n4,
    196n7
Cyrus, 107, 172

Dagon, 116–17, 122
Dan, 59, 100, 165, 182, 197n16

Daniel, 35, 106
David, 21, 27, 35, 43–45, 61, 66,
    68, 70, 108, 123, 126–27, 159,
    160, 161, 169, 170, 185
Dead Sea, 29, 55–56, 59, 61, 62,
    68
Dead Sea Scrolls, 29, 62
death, 24, 80–81, 121, 173–82
death penalty, 146–47
Deborah, 168–69
Delilah, 21

Eden, 23, 24, 79, 123
Egypt, 25, 34, 42, 54, 58, 61,
    93–98, 104, 113–16, 120, 125,
    134–35, 141, 152–56, 167, 174
Ehud, 40, 51
El, 101, 109–11
Elijah, 44, 119, 120, 164, 178,
    183
Esau, 40
Esther, 38, 107
Euphrates, River, 55, 61, 79, 88,
    98, 103
Eve, 23, 24, 77–82, 87, 112, 175,
    185
exodus, the, 25, 34, 97–98,
    115–16, 118, 160, 197n3,
    200n2

family, 34, 111, 139–41, 144–47,
    176–77

Galilee, Sea of, 55, 59–61, 63
Gerar, 18
Gibeah, 160
Gideon, 47
Gilgamesh, 89, 175, 201nn1–2

Gomorrah, 62
Goshen, 54, 152

Hadad, 116
Ham, 98, 100, 101
Haran, 82, 85
Hazor, 99, 100, 104, 157, 161, 162,
    169
Hermon, Mount, 59
Hezekiah, 96, 104, 169, 170
Hittites, 54, 57, 98, 102, 167
Hyksos, 96, 97

Isaac, 35, 40–42, 46, 110, 118–19, 139

Jacob, 35, 42, 97, 110, 111, 176
Jebusites, 100, 101, 160
Jehu, 103
Jephthah, 111–12
Jeremiah, 96, 113, 145, 185
Jericho, 20, 62, 63, 78, 88, 99,
    100, 156, 157, 159, 183
Jerusalem, 43, 60–61, 96, 101,
    104, 127, 129, 159, 161–62,
    169–70, 172, 184
Jesus, 20, 30, 61, 70, 85, 110, 122,
    128, 129, 132–33, 136, 138, 140,
    148–49, 177, 182, 186–87
Jezreel, 57, 60
Job, 179, 182
Jonah, 35–36, 43, 104–5
Jordan, River, 55, 56, 59, 61, 62,
    156, 160
Joseph, 42, 95, 97, 145, 176
Joshua, 102, 118, 156, 157
Jubilee, 141–44
judge, 27, 42, 47, 111–12, 120,
    144, 166, 168, 193n1

Kadesh, 18
kingdom, 9, 103–4, 160, 184
king. *See* monarchy.
Kiriath Jearim, 43

Lachish, 104, 171–72
language, 17, 78, 83, 89–90, 92,
    93, 99, 100, 105, 106
law, 20, 43, 45, 46, 80, 124–26,
    132–49, 178, 185–86, 200n5,
    200n8
Lebanon, 66

Mamre, 21
manuscripts, 29
marriage, 139–41, 162
Masada, 62
Mediterranean Sea, 54, 59, 60,
    61, 90, 102, 105, 117
Megiddo, 57, 60, 161, 162, 169
Melchizedek, 101, 102
metalwork, 26, 78, 97, 102,
    166–67
miracles, 22–23, 36, 61, 155
Moab, 40, 50, 112, 159
Molech, 117–19, 121, 122
monarchy, 45, 47, 63, 77, 94, 96,
    99, 107, 139, 144–45, 160,
    162–63, 166–67, 177
Mordecai, 38
Moriah, Mount, 40–41, 118, 127
Moses, 25, 58–59, 75–76, 110, 116,
    125, 126, 132, 152, 155, 183,
    185, 200n1
music, 78, 83, 90, 99, 106, 120,
    183
mythology, 21–23, 33, 70–71,
    114, 120

Naphtali, 59, 162
Nathan, 35
Nazareth, 60
Negev, 18, 59
Nile, River, 54, 55–56, 61, 88, 95,
    113–14
Nineveh, 104–5
Noah, 49, 70, 101, 175

Omri, 103

Passover 34, 193n1 (chap. 2)
Paul, apostle, 17, 71, 113, 137,
    138, 141, 182, 193n2
Persians, 27, 38, 107–8
Philistines 26, 57, 60, 102–3, 108,
    116–17, 153, 162, 165, 166, 167,
    168
Phoenicians, 56, 60, 117
pyramid, 25, 89, 91, 94–95, 98,
    105, 152

Qumran, 29, 62

Rachel, 111
Rameses, 98, 126, 153, 168
Red Sea, (Sea of Reeds), 55,
    153–56, 167
roads, 57, 90, 100, 153, 155, 159,
    170
Rosetta Stone, 93

Sabbath, 133–34, 142–43, 149
Samson, 21, 47, 66
Sarah, 42, 176, 185
Satan, 79, 121–23, 193n2
Saul, 68, 116, 160, 166, 178
Shur, 18

Sinai, Mount, 156
slavery, 98, 134, 146, 148, 152, 175
Sodom, 62, 194–95n2
soldiers, 56, 57, 144, 166, 168, 170
Solomon, 59, 96, 97, 107, 119, 127,
    144–45, 161–63, 169, 170
Sumerians, 55, 82–83, 88–92,
    167, 175, 198n6

tabernacle, 46, 76, 125–29, 161,
    167, 182, 199n14
temple, 92, 94, 97, 105, 106, 107,
    116–17, 126–29, 144, 158, 182

Terah, 82, 92
Tigris, River, 55–56, 79, 88, 103

Ur, 82–83, 85, 89–92
Uruk, 89, 175, 201n1
Uzzah, 43

warfare, 26, 57–58, 90, 97, 104,
    156–58, 165–72
writing, 25, 46, 83, 89, 90, 94, 95, 194n7

Zedekiah, 145
ziggurat, 89, 91–92, 94, 105